T0358612

Managing Healthcare Projects Using DSDM and Agile Project Management

Managing Healthcare Projects Using DSDM and Agile Project Management: A Comprehensive Guide for Professionals provides a comprehensive guide to implementing agile project management (Agile PM) in healthcare.

Dynamic systems development method (DSDM) is an agile project delivery framework initially used as a software development method and was originally sought to provide some discipline to the rapid application development method. Agile PM is a method that emphasises flexibility, cooperation, and iterative development, which can be especially useful in healthcare where rapid adaptability to changing circumstances is required. Traditional project management methodologies may not always be appropriate in the healthcare industry due to unique obstacles and constraints. This book addresses these issues and offers practical advice on how to use agile ideas and practices in healthcare projects. It covers a variety of topics, all specialised to the healthcare environment, such as project planning, stakeholder involvement, risk management, and quality assurance. Healthcare organisations are increasingly recognising the value of agility in thriving in a competitive market and meeting the changing requirements of patients and staff. Agile PM has been proved in several industries to improve efficiency, stakeholder satisfaction, and overall project outcomes. Agility is critical in the healthcare sector in particular for effectively responding to crises like as the COVID-19 epidemic and enabling the development of Healthcare 4.0.

This book is an excellent resource for healthcare workers looking to embrace Agile PM practices. Its focus on healthcare and practical instruction set it apart and makes it relevant to the demands of the industry. Adopting agile methodologies allows healthcare organisations to improve project outcomes, increase stakeholder satisfaction, and effectively respond to the industry's dynamic problems.

Managing Healthcare Projects Using DSDM and Agile Project Management

A Comprehensive Guide for Professionals

Oswin Kakumanu

Routledge
Taylor & Francis Group

A PRODUCTIVITY PRESS BOOK

Designed cover image: Shutterstock

First published 2025
by Routledge
605 Third Avenue, New York, NY 10158

and by Routledge
4 Park Square, Milton Park, Abingdon, Oxon, OX14 4RN

Routledge is an imprint of the Taylor & Francis Group, an informa business

ISBN: 978-1-032-68842-8 (hbk)
ISBN: 978-1-032-68841-1 (pbk)
ISBN: 978-1-032-68843-5 (ebk)

DOI: 10.4324/9781032688435

Typeset in Adobe Garamond
by KnowledgeWorks Global Ltd.

Contents

About the Author

Oswin Kakumanu is currently the PMO Delivery Lead (South Island) for the Integration and Delivery Subfunction within the Data & Digital Business Unit of Health New Zealand. He also serves as the PMO Manager for the Digital Transformation Programme of the New Dunedin Hospital. With 25 years of international experience in various P3M management roles, Oswin has built the capabilities of over 3,000 professionals in countries such as New Zealand, Australia, United Arab Emirates, Saudi Arabia, Qatar, Bahrain, and Oman in diverse management disciplines, including portfolio, programme, project, PMO, business case, change, and agile management. He worked with organisations, such as Deloitte, Accenture, Novartis, and Booz Allen Hamilton.

Oswin is a certified Project Management Professional (PMP) and Program Management Professional (PgMP) from the Project Management Institute (PMI), United States. He holds PRINCE2, MSP, MoP, M_o_R, and P3O practitioner certifications from Axelos. Additionally, Oswin is an agile project management (Agile PM) certified professional and holds Praxis Practitioner, Better Business Cases Practitioner, and Change Management Practitioner certifications from APMG International.

Oswin's academic achievements include three master's degrees: an MBA from Murdoch University, Australia; a Master of Applied Management from the Southern Institute of Technology, New Zealand; and a Master of Business (Finance) from Lincoln University, New Zealand. He has also completed a bachelor's in applied management from Otago Polytechnic, New Zealand. He is expected to complete his doctoral studies in business administration from the Otago Business School, University of Otago, in 2024.

Foreword

In the healthcare sector, achieving patient outcomes is a key measure of success. In the context of disruptive innovation, focus on patient safety, ethical considerations, multidisciplinary collaboration, and demand for stronger regulation and compliance. Organisations, industry, and governments that deliver healthcare services and products are looking at the efficacy of projects and programmes they invest in. Stakeholders have expressed predictive and adaptive needs in the way projects are managed and delivered, and project practices are evolving to meet these needs.

In this book, Oswin spotlights the dynamic systems development method (DSDM) in the healthcare context and makes a compelling case for its suitability and adoption. He delves into the intricacies of managing projects using this methodology with examples, scenarios, and case studies with practical guidance that project professionals will find useful and a welcome addition to their toolkit.

Part I lays the foundation; it introduces readers to DSDM and agile methodologies. By understanding the principles of DSDM to exploring key agile practices, readers are equipped with the necessary tools to embark on their agile journey.

Part II delves into the practical implementation of DSDM and agile in healthcare projects. From preparing organisations for agile adoption to initiating and planning projects using DSDM, each chapter offers practical insights and actionable strategies for success.

Part III explores advanced topics and case studies, offering real-world examples of healthcare projects managed using DSDM and agile methodologies. From scaling agile in larger projects to managing risks and compliance considerations, readers gain a holistic understanding of agile project management in the healthcare context.

As the healthcare landscape continues to evolve, embracing agility and adaptability becomes imperative. Through *Managing Healthcare Projects Using DSDM and Agile Project Management*, Oswin empowers project professionals in healthcare to navigate the complexities of the industry with confidence, where patient-centricity and innovation reign supreme.

I commend Oswin for his insightful exploration of healthcare project management and advocacy for the adoption of DSDM and agile methodologies. May this guide serve as a beacon for project professionals seeking to transform healthcare delivery and improve patient outcomes.

■ Geoffrey Henderson, Senior Project and Programme Management Professional, New Zealand

Preface

In the ever-changing environment of healthcare, where innovation and regulation meet, good project management is critical. Healthcare projects are more than just delivering products or services; they are about improving patient outcomes, improving care delivery, and, ultimately, saving lives. However, the sector's specific problems, including complicated regulatory frameworks, various stakeholders, and ongoing pressure to adapt to new technologies and treatments, necessitate a project management approach that is both resilient and adaptable.

This book, *Managing Healthcare Projects Using DSDM and Agile Project Management*, provides a complete guide to traversing this complex terrain. It exposes you to the dynamic systems development method (DSDM) and agile techniques, two powerful frameworks that have proven effective in delivering successful projects across a variety of industries, including healthcare. Understanding and applying the principles and practices discussed in this book will prepare you to lead healthcare initiatives that not only meet but exceed expectations.

Whether you are a seasoned healthcare project manager looking to expand your skill set or a beginner eager to make a difference in this crucial industry, this book will provide you with the knowledge and tools you need to succeed. We will look at the special issues of healthcare project management, go over the foundations of DSDM and agile, and provide practical advice on how to apply these approaches in real-world healthcare settings. Case studies and examples will provide you with useful insights into how these frameworks have been effectively used to improve patient care, streamline operations, and drive innovation in healthcare organisations throughout the world.

This book is more than just a theoretical treatise; it is a practical manual that will equip you to make a significant influence in the healthcare business. By embracing the ideas of DSDM and agile, you will be able to lead projects that are not just efficient and successful but also truly patient-centred and sensitive to the healthcare landscape's ever-changing requirements. We welcome you to embark on this adventure of learning and discovery, and to help shape the future of healthcare project management.

Introduction

The Unique Challenges and Complexities of Healthcare Project Management

The healthcare industry is distinguished from many others by its complex network of rules, fast expanding technologies, and profound impact on the lives of patients and communities. These characteristics create a distinct landscape for healthcare project management, where success requires more than simply technical project knowledge.

Healthcare project managers must handle a complex environment that includes:

Regulatory compliance: Strict rules aimed at protecting patient safety and privacy (such as Health Insurance Portability and Accountability Act [HIPPA] and General Data Protection Regulation [GDPR], and local requirements) complicate project workflows and deliverables. Let me give you a couple of examples:

Example 1: Setting up a new electronic health record (EHR) system – Strict restrictions (HIPAA in the United States) control the storage, transmission, and use of patient information. An EHR installation project must involve safe data migration, privacy protocol training for clinicians, and regular compliance audits.

The Cleveland Clinic: Any major hospital's transition to a new EHR system, such as the Cleveland Clinic's to Epic, is a massive operation that requires HIPAA-compliant security and patient privacy to be successful.

Example 2: Create a clinical decision support tool – Regulations governing the use of algorithms and AI in healthcare require detailed documentation of the tool's design, validation processes, and steps to assure patient safety and eliminate biases.

Dr. John Halamka is an advocate for interoperability and health information technology, and he has talked extensively about the regulatory challenges of EHRs, drawing on his experience at Beth Israel Deaconess Medical Centre and as CIO of Mayo Clinic.

Multidisciplinary collaboration: Healthcare initiatives frequently involve various teams of clinicians, administrators, IT specialists, and external suppliers, each with their own set of specialised skills and priorities. Effective teamwork is critical, but it can be hampered by communication gaps and compartmentalised working patterns. Let me illustrate with a couple of examples:

Example 1: Redesigning an emergency department workflow – Clinicians, nurses, administrators, facilities personnel, and possibly IT specialists must collaborate. Each group has its own priorities. Effective communication and conflict resolution are critical to achieving a solution that benefits all stakeholders.

Kaiser Permanente: Known for its integrated health system, their ED redesign initiatives would logically incorporate multidisciplinary teams to achieve the best results.

Emergency Medicine Physician Groups: Groups such as American College of Emergency Physicians (ACEP) frequently exchange case studies and best practices in which teamwork improved ED efficiency.

Example 2: Partnering with a medical device company – A project to install a novel surgical device includes hospital procurement, clinician training, device engineers, and the company's regulatory affairs experts. Coordinating timetables, technical standards, and regulatory understanding necessitates extensive collaborative preparation.

Johnson & Johnson's medical device division works with hospitals on device implementation initiatives, which require expertise on both sides to overcome regulations and achieve adoption.

Hospital procurement leaders: These often unseen professionals play critical roles in device projects, balancing clinical needs with cost and regulatory constraints.

Ethical considerations: Healthcare projects have ethical implications since decisions affect patient well-being and resource allocation. Project managers must strike a balance between innovation and improvement while remaining ethically responsible for patients and healthcare resources. Let me provide you with a couple of examples:

Example 1: Implementing a telehealth platform – While telehealth improves access to care, it raises concerns about equity for underprivileged people (technical gaps, language obstacles). Project design should incorporate techniques for addressing potential inequities.

The Center for Connected Health Policy: This non-profit specialises in telehealth policy, and their programmes demonstrate a focus on increasing access while addressing health disparity.

Patient advocate groups: Organisations representing marginalised populations frequently voice critical concerns about telehealth programmes to ensure that vulnerable patient groups are not further disadvantaged.

Example 2: Resource allocation for rare disease research – Research funding decisions must strike a balance between the quest of novel cures for rare diseases and the need to address prevalent health disorders that affect a wider population. Ethical frameworks serve to guide project prioritisation.

National Organization for Rare Disorders (NORD): This organisation plays a significant role in financing decisions and ethical recommendations for rare illness research.

Abby Meyers, the XDP Project's founder, is a strong champion for the rapid discovery of medicines for ultra-rare diseases as well as a patient.

Constant evolution: Medical advancements, technological upheavals, and shifting health legislation all contribute to an ever-changing world. Healthcare projects must be flexible in order to remain relevant and effective. Let me provide a couple of examples:

Example 1: Adapting to new treatment guidelines – Clinical trials and medical research are constantly updating best practices in care. Projects that include upgrading clinical pathways or training materials must have means for quickly incorporating the most recent findings.

National Comprehensive Cancer Network (NCCN): Their often revised guidelines influence cancer treatment, necessitating that hospitals have adaptive procedures in place for sharing this knowledge.

Chief medical information officers (CMIOs): These experts frequently lead projects aimed at maintaining clinical pathways and decision support tools up to date within their health systems.

Example 2: Upgrading cybersecurity protocols – The increase of cyberthreats in healthcare necessitates continuous security enhancements. Projects may entail adopting new encryption methods or providing staff training, necessitating adaptability to face emerging threats.

NIST developed the Healthcare Sector Cybersecurity Framework, which highlights the industry's specialised cybersecurity demands as well as the shifting nature of threat protection.

HITRUST: This organisation focusses on healthcare-specific cybersecurity standards, requiring projects to be adaptive as those standards change.

Human-centred focus: Patient outcomes and experiences are important to healthcare. Project managers must prioritise patient-centred solutions while maintaining operational efficiencies. Let me illustrate with a couple of examples:

Example 1: Designing a patient portal – Features like appointment scheduling, test results access, and medicine refills must be user-friendly for patients with varied levels of technological knowledge. A truly patient-centric approach must include user feedback obtained through testing.

Mayo Clinic Centre for Innovation is noted for its patient-centred design, and their patient portal initiatives are likely to entail extensive user participation.

Don Norman, author of *The Design of Everyday Things*, believes that human-centred design concepts are essential for every patient-facing technology initiative.

Example 2: Improving hospital discharge processes – Collaborating with social services and community care providers is frequently required to reduce readmissions. To ensure a successful discharge plan, the project must look beyond the hospital's walls and address a patient's overall needs.

The SCAN Foundation focuses on challenges affecting seniors, frequently sponsoring programmes that address care transitions, where collaboration and comprehensive patient assessments are critical.

Hospital case managers: They are on the front lines, enabling discharge, and their views are crucial for truly patient-centred process improvement initiatives.

Let me further provide you with three scenarios with real-world examples to illustrate why traditional project management systems frequently fall short of addressing the abovementioned difficulties.

Scenario 1: Strict Planning and Changing Regulations

Traditional approach: A project to modernise a hospital's billing system is planned using a thorough, linear Gantt chart, with a lengthy planning phase followed by implementation. Midway through the project, laws surrounding reimbursement codes change. Adapting necessitates extensive rework or perhaps scrapping huge areas, resulting in delays and cost overruns.

The shortcoming: Traditional models struggle with large mid-course revisions as the healthcare regulatory landscape changes.

Let me provide you with a real-world example:

The ACA Rollout with Healthcare.gov (US example): The initial implementation of the Affordable Care Act website was plagued by problems due to inflexible planning, limited scalability, and difficulties adapting to changing rules during the project's life cycle. It is a classic example of the high costs of linear project management in a dynamic healthcare policy context.

Scenario 2: Siloed Teams and Inefficient Workflows

Traditional approach: A new patient scheduling system is being implemented. IT performs software installation, followed by a second team that provides user training. Clinicians are not involved early enough, resulting in workflow problems and unhappiness after adoption.

The shortcoming: Traditional approaches with consecutive hand-offs may miss important information. Lack of cross-functional collaboration from the start reduces the system's efficacy and adoption.

Let me provide you with a real-world example:

NHS (UK example): The NHS has long been criticised for segregated departments (IT, clinical teams, etc.), which result in unproductive initiatives. A notorious example was a multimillion-pound national patient record system that failed due to insufficient communication and collaboration among parties.

Scenario 3: Prioritising the Project Over Patient Outcomes

Traditional approach: A project to establish a new drug management system is heavily focused on technical milestones and timely, on-budget delivery. A lack of focus on how it affects clinician workflows results in a technically successful system but increased clinical irritation and the possibility of compromising patient safety.

The shortcoming: Traditional techniques often overemphasise task completion, leaving out the wider picture of how the project affects patient care and experience.

Let me provide you with a general example:

Hospital workflow redesign initiatives (General): Projects aimed at streamlining processes to enhance efficiency frequently succeed on paper (saving time and money), but fail because clinician involvement is insufficient. Staff may devise workarounds to counteract the new process, or the patient experience may deteriorate owing to unforeseen consequences.

Traditional project management systems frequently fall short of addressing the abovementioned difficulties, and we have seen that illustrated in the three scenarios above. This book introduces the dynamic systems development method (DSDM) and agile techniques as effective frameworks for healthcare project managers. Their emphasis on flexibility, cooperation, and continual development is consistent with the dynamic and value-driven nature of healthcare projects.

The Need for Agility and Adaptability in Healthcare Projects

The healthcare landscape is in constant motion. Breakthrough medical discoveries, changing regulations, altering patient expectations, and rapid technological improvements are reshaping the way healthcare is delivered. In this dynamic environment, traditional project management approaches with inflexible planning and sequential execution are frequently ineffective. Healthcare projects necessitate a distinct mindset – one that values agility and adaptability as its foundation.

Agility relates to a project's ability to react quickly to change, pivot directions, and adapt to changing conditions. Adaptability refers to the ability to change workflows, realign priorities, and modify solutions in response to new requirements or unanticipated obstacles. These characteristics are important in healthcare because of considerations like:

The pace of innovation: New pharmaceuticals, medical technologies, and treatment methods demand a project management style that can easily accommodate such improvements. Let me further illustrate this with a couple of examples:

Example 1: COVID-19 vaccine development – The quick development of COVID-19 vaccines necessitated unparalleled agility. Projects included shortening timescales, running parallel research tracks, and quickly adjusting manufacturing processes when new data regarding variants became available. Traditional project management could not have kept up.

Example 2: Robotic surgery implementation – As robotic surgical systems improve, hospitals that embrace this technology require a project management methodology that can handle upgrades, new staff training modules, and process changes. A rigorous plan would quickly become obsolete.

Let us also provide you with a couple of real-world examples:

Dr. Katalin Karikó is a key researcher behind the mRNA technology utilised in COVID-19 vaccinations. Her decades of perseverance in the face of scepticism and disappointments in her studies demonstrate the unexpected nature of medical innovation. Agile project management (Agile PM) in such research must be prepared for restarts, direction changes, and rapid acceleration when breakthroughs are discovered.

Moderna: Despite being a very young firm, Moderna was able to quickly pivot and produce one of the first mRNA COVID-19 vaccines thanks to previous flexible and iterative research methodologies, demonstrating the value of agility in drug development.

Unpredictability: Healthcare can be unpredictable, with changing disease trends or public health crises necessitating flexibility in resource allocation and project prioritisation. Let me provide with a couple of examples:

Example 1: Pandemic response – The COVID-19 pandemic compelled hospitals to quickly reprioritise projects. Elective treatments were postponed, urgent telemedicine initiatives were expedited, and facilities were adapted to handle increases in patient demand. This necessitated significantly more flexibility than standard project methodologies.

Example 2: Natural catastrophe planning – While hospitals have catastrophe protocols, the nature of the occurrences (hurricanes, earthquakes, etc.) necessitates special considerations. Project designs must be flexible enough to adjust to the types of resources, infrastructure damage, and patient care that are required.

Let me provide a couple of real-world examples to illustrate further:

Médecins Sans Frontières (Doctors Without Borders): This worldwide humanitarian organisation typically works in uncertain situations, giving care during conflicts, epidemics, and natural disasters. Their initiatives necessitate rapid mobilisation, adaptability to resource changes, and continual reassessment – all characteristics of agile thinking.

Partners in health is a nonprofit organisation dedicated to providing high-quality care in low-income communities. Their projects frequently involve unforeseen elements such as political unrest or supply chain interruptions. Agile techniques, with revisions as needed, are critical to success in satisfying community demands.

Stakeholder needs: The different demands of patients, physicians, administrators, and regulatory authorities must be balanced while ensuring project objectives are consistent with providing quality treatment. Let me illustrate this with examples:

Example 1: Wearable health monitoring implementation – Introducing wearable devices for chronic disease monitoring necessitates support from patients (ensuring ease of use), clinicians (trusting data accuracy), and IT (addressing data security). An agile approach that incorporates feedback loops from each of these groups is required for success.

Example 2: Addressing health disparities – A project aimed at improving health outcomes in marginalised communities must strike a balance between the needs of community outreach workers, clinicians modifying care delivery methods, and potentially local government entities seeking regulatory and funding assistance. Agile cooperation is critical for delivering a solution that meets everyone's requirements.

Let me further illustrate with real-world examples:

Patient advocate groups: People living with conditions (such as the Cystic Fibrosis Foundation) have important voices that influence research goals. Their feedback is crucial in designing agile healthcare projects that ensure outcomes fit with real patient needs rather than just clinical goals.

The Mayo Clinic Centre for Innovation focusses on changing healthcare delivery. Their projects involve patients as active partners in co-designing solutions for improved care experiences, reflecting the multi-stakeholder collaboration inherent in agile methodology.

Healthcare organisations that rely on rigid project approaches run the danger of missing deadlines, incurring cost overruns, and implementing solutions that are out of sync with reality. This book presents DSDM and agile approaches as revolutionary frameworks for healthcare project management. Their emphasis on iterative development, collaboration, and putting user value first aligns with the healthcare sector's ever-changing needs.

The Benefits of Using DSDM and Agile Methodologies in the Healthcare Context

The complexity of healthcare necessitates project management approaches that extend beyond the rigidity of standard frameworks. DSDM and agile approaches provide a compelling solution that reflects the dynamic, patient-centred, and collaborative character of healthcare delivery. Adopting these frameworks allows healthcare organisations to reap major benefits, including:

Enhanced adaptability: Agile methodologies, with their iterative approach and emphasis on constant feedback, enable projects to embrace change and quickly adapt to the changing healthcare sector. This allows for the timely integration of new research findings, regulatory developments, and responses to evolving public health requirements.
NHS Digital (UK): They've started using agile methodologies on projects like establishing national health data systems. This enables them to more effectively respond to changes in health policy and technology.
Partners in health: Their approach to the Ebola crisis in West Africa is an excellent example of adaptation. Their work on the ground most likely used agile approaches (albeit not expressly stated), as they altered care practices and resource allocation as the outbreak progressed.

Improved collaboration: DSDM and agile place an emphasis on cross-functional teamwork. This eliminates silos among clinicians, IT, administrators, and patients. This collaboration generates more effective solutions that meet the needs of all stakeholders.
Geisinger health system is known for its innovative treatment models, and they have embraced agile techniques to facilitate collaboration between physicians and data scientists in the development of predictive analytics tools.
Intermountain healthcare: They used Agile PM principles to construct clinical decision support tools, encouraging active participation from physicians and IT teams.

Prioritised patient value: Patient-centricity is a fundamental principle of both DSDM and agile. The emphasis moves from just completing projects to ensuring that the deliverables actually improve the patient experience and promote health and well-being.
The Mayo Clinic Centre for Innovation frequently collaborates with patients on their ideas. This agile methodology ensures that healthcare solutions are truly responsive to patients' requirements.
Dr. Eric Topol (from Scripps Research): Aside from campaigning for AI in medicine, he also promotes patient-centred design, which aligns with agile's emphasis on the end-user perspective.

Accelerated innovation: The ability to successfully manage change and incorporate stakeholder feedback leads to faster, more efficient development. This can be critical in fields such as medical device development and digital health solutions, where the rate of innovation affects patient care.
Roche (Pharmaceutical) has used agile frameworks in drug development to shorten research cycles and react to new discoveries as they arise.
Babylon Health (Digital Healthcare): Their rapid development of AI-powered symptom checkers and telehealth services demonstrates the potential of agile approaches for providing timely healthcare solutions.

Risk reduction: The iterative structure of DSDM and agile projects enables early risk detection and mitigation. It avoids the costly problems of discovering significant compliance concerns or user discontent late in the typical project lifecycle.

U.S. Food and Drug Administration (FDA) case studies: The FDA has case studies on employing iterative development methodologies (similar to agile) for medical device software, which promotes early detection of safety hazards.

Hospital's Chief Information Security Officer (CISO): Individuals in this job frequently push for agile-style methodologies in security projects due to the ever-changing threat landscape, where early risk detection is critical.

This book delves into the practical application of DSDM and agile principles in a variety of healthcare projects, illustrating how these approaches improve project outcomes, efficiency, and, ultimately, patient care.

FUNDAMENTALS OF DSDM AND AGILE

Chapter 1

Introduction to DSDM

Overview of the Dynamic Systems Development Method (DSDM) and Its Principles

What Is DSDM?

The dynamic systems development method (DSDM) is an agile project delivery framework built expressly to meet the issues of projects with unknown requirements that are likely to alter throughout development. DSDM emphasises cooperation, iterative development, frequent value delivery, and fitness for business purpose. Let us break this down further:

a. "Agile" framework: DSDM belongs to a larger family of agile techniques. This means it shares fundamental ideas such as adaptability, constant improvement, and prioritising customer (or stakeholder) satisfaction.
b. "Managing uncertainty": Traditional project management generally believes that the majority of needs can be defined in advance. DSDM recognises that many initiatives (particularly those in healthcare) develop as they progress.
c. "Iterative development": DSDM projects divide work into smaller portions rather than delivering it all at once. You offer useable sections rapidly, solicit feedback, and utilise it to shape the next iteration.
d. "Frequent delivery of value": This does not simply imply delivering something; it also involves delivering something that stakeholders find actually beneficial. It fosters trust and ensures that the final solution meets real demands.
e. "Fitness for business purpose": DSDM emphasises that it is more than just a technical deliverable. It is important to ensure that whatever is produced actively supports the organisation's goals (such as enhancing patient outcomes and efficiency).

Analogy: Consider traditional project management as building a house from a comprehensive blueprint. DSDM is similar to an interior designer remodelling a room: There is a general vision of the desired outcome, but choices and adjustments are made along the process based on what works in the space and what the client prefers.

DOI: 10.4324/9781032688435-2

Historical Context

a. **The limits of "waterfall"**: Prior to DSDM, many projects depended significantly on the "waterfall" paradigm. This indicates that tasks are completed in a sequential order: requirements collecting, design, programming, testing, and deployment. This was stiff and unsuited to shifting needs.

b. The 1990s saw **the rise of rapid application development (RAD)**, which included DSDM. RAD emphasised bringing working versions of software in front of users as soon as possible so that they could provide feedback and tweak the product as necessary.

c. **DSDM's formation**: In 1994, a group of RAD practitioners recognised the need for additional structure and governance in this iterative process. This resulted in the construction of the initial version of DSDM.

d. **Software and beyond**: DSDM was first designed to address the fast-paced nature of the software business. However, its essential ideas have proven adaptable to a variety of projects where flexibility and stakeholder participation are critical.

e. **DSDM Atern**: The most current iteration, DSDM Atern (or just Atern), demonstrates the framework's ongoing adaption to new project management trends and technology.

Why This Matters in Healthcare

■ **Healthcare has similar challenges**: Much like software in the 1990s, healthcare is constantly developing. Projects typically cannot afford the extensive upfront planning required by traditional approaches and must learn as they go.

■ **A proven approach**: DSDM is not an unproven notion. It's a structure that's been perfected over decades, making it a dependable option for dealing with the complexities of healthcare initiatives.

Key Principles of DSDM

DSDM is founded upon eight core principles that guide project execution and decision-making:

1. Focus on the business need: Prioritising the delivery of real value to stakeholders throughout the project.

   Example 1: Hospital electronic health record (EHR) implementation – A hospital wants more than simply new software; it wants to improve patient care and operational efficiency. A DSDM project would conduct regular assessments to ensure that the system being developed is truly supporting those end goals, rather than simply providing feature checklists.

   Example 2: Public health initiatives – When tackling a health condition such as diabetes, programmes should not just record activities (e.g., workshops held) but provide true value. A DSDM strategy focuses on tracking the true impact on health outcomes in the community.

2. Deliver on time: Emphasis on meeting deadlines and delivering working increments of the solution frequently.

   Example 1: Medical device development – Delays can lead to a competitor entering the market first. DSDM's timeboxing helps fulfil deadlines by delivering fundamental functions initially, with expanded functionality potentially coming later.

Example 2: Dr. Atul Gawande, surgeon and author – He believes that checklists can help surgeons achieve better results. This is consistent with DSDM's focus on producing viable solutions rapidly and developing them over time.

3. Collaborate: Fostering a collaborative environment between stakeholders, users, and the development team.

   Example 1: Renovations at a community clinic have an influence on patients, doctors, nurses, and administrative staff. Instead of relying solely on architects and builders to drive the process, DSDM would actively involve all of these organisations.

   Example 2: Patient advocacy groups – They frequently have a thorough understanding of what a truly beneficial digital health solution might look like. DSDM emphasises collaboration with such organisations from the outset, rather than just asking for feedback at the end.

4. Never compromise quality: Maintaining high standards for quality and ensuring that deliverables are fit for purpose.

   Example 1: FDA regulations require software for medical devices to meet stringent quality criteria. DSDM does not forsake thorough testing; rather, it structures it within iterations, allowing issues to be identified early on.

   Example 2: Clinical trial management – DSDM programmes that manage trial data would engage statisticians and quality control professionals at all stages to assure data integrity and trustworthy outcomes.

5. Build incrementally from firm foundations: Iterative development approach starting with a strong foundation and continuously adding features and value.

   Example 1: Telehealth platform – A DSDM project may prioritise secure video visits and messaging. Once the fundamental system is stable, features such as AI-powered triage could be added in subsequent versions.

   Example 2: Hospital workflow changes – Re-imagining the entire ER process is difficult. DSDM could split it down into steps, such as enhancing patient intake, bed allocation, and so forth.

6. Communicate continuously and clearly: Transparent and open communication amongst all stakeholders is essential.

   Example 1: Disease outbreak response – Public health organisations must send frequent updates to the public and healthcare professionals. DSDM's emphasis on transparency contributes to rapid and accurate information dissemination.

   Example 2: Shared decision-making – Healthcare is increasingly involving patients in their treatment decisions. This idea encourages transparent communication in order to allow empowered patient decision-making.

7. Demonstrate control: Implementing processes to manage project progress, risks, and changes proactively.

   Example 1: Cybersecurity incident – Healthcare is not immune to hacks. A DSDM methodology prepares for such eventualities by conducting frequent risk assessments and developing incident response plans, ensuring proactive control even in the face of uncertainty.

   Example 2: Clinical pathways define the best techniques for treating certain illnesses. To control variances in care delivery, DSDM-style management guarantees that they are reviewed and updated on a regular basis using the most recent evidence.

8. Focus on fitness for business purpose: Ensuring that the delivered solution truly meets the business need and aligns with operational goals.

Example 1: New wearable device – In addition to technical success, a wearable project should be evaluated to see if it increases patient adherence to medicine or lifestyle modifications, thereby supporting the healthcare organisation's health outcomes goals.

Example 2: Rare disease research – Projects must be evaluated based on their impact on patients with certain disorders, even if the patient population is small, to demonstrate alignment with the organisation's purpose of care.

DSDM in the Healthcare Context

DSDM is especially suitable for healthcare initiatives because of the following:

■ Adapting to regulatory change.

Scenario: Midway through a project to establish a clinical data reporting system, a change occurs in how certain metrics must be presented to agencies such as the U.S. Centers for Disease Control and Prevention (CDC).

DSDM's iterative approach and emphasis on early stakeholder feedback enable the project to course correct, as opposed to traditional models where rework would be extensive and costly.

■ Accommodating increasing research and treatment possibilities.

Scenario: A project focused on building care pathways for a difficult disease discovers potential new medication trials in the middle of development.

DSDM is not based on a fixed plan. Feedback loops and iterative delivery enable the integration of new results into the pathway, ensuring that it represents the most recent best practices.

■ Prioritising patient-centred design and engagement with healthcare experts.

Scenario: A new patient portal is technically working, but clinicians and patients find it difficult to navigate.

DSDM involves patients and physicians throughout the design process. Issues are identified early on, avoiding an expensive failure after full launch.

The DSDM Project Lifecycle and Phases

The DSDM process model includes a framework that depicts the DSDM stages and their relationships to one another (Figure 1.1). Each project uses this process model to determine its lifespan.

Pre-project phase: The pre-project phase ensures that only the appropriate projects are initiated and that they are properly set up, with a clearly defined aim.

Feasibility phase: The feasibility phase is primarily meant to determine whether the proposed project is technically feasible and appears cost-effective from a business standpoint. The work required for feasibility should be sufficient to determine if additional inquiry is warranted or whether the project should be halted immediately because it is unlikely to be viable.

Foundations phase: The foundations phase advances the exploratory inquiry beyond the feasibility stage. It is meant to provide a fundamental (but not extensive) understanding of the project's business justification, potential solution, and how development and delivery of the solution will be managed. The phase, which purposely avoids low levels of detail, should last no more than a few weeks, even for huge and complex projects. The details of requirements

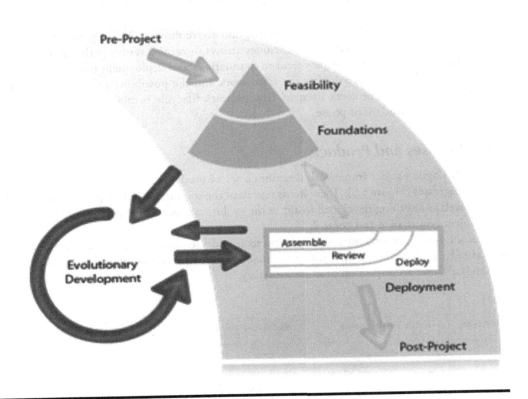

Figure 1.1   DSDM project lifecycle and phases.

and how they should be addressed as part of the solution are purposely deferred until the project's evolutionary development phase. The goal of foundations is to comprehend the scope of work and, in general, how it will be carried out, who will do it, when, and where. The phase also establishes the project lifecycle by agreeing on how the DSDM method will be applied to the project's specific requirements. For smaller, simpler projects, the feasibility and foundations phases can sometimes be combined into a single one. For larger, more complicated projects, it may be required to examine foundations following each deployment step.

The evolutionary development phase aims to evolve the solution by building on the project's solid foundations. During the evolutionary development phase, the solution development team(s) must use practices such as iterative development, timeboxing, and MoSCoW prioritisation, as well as modelling and facilitated workshops, to converge over time on an accurate solution that meets the business need while also being built correctly from a technical standpoint. The solution development team works within timeboxes to build solution increments, iteratively examining the low-level detail of the requirements and continuously testing as they progress.

The goal of the **deployment phase** is to bring a baseline of the evolving solution into practical use. The release that is deployed could be the ultimate solution or a subset of the ultimate solution. Following the final release, the project is formally closed.

Post-project phase: Following the final deployment of a project, the post-project phase assesses how effectively the predicted business benefits were met.

Lifecycle in practice: While the process diagram above shows a clear sequence of phases from pre-project to post-project, it also includes arrows showing a return path inside the process, notably the arrows from deployment to foundations and deployment to evolutionary development. The procedure depicts the framework and the possibilities accessible. This procedure defines each project's lifespan. The project's lifecycle is established and agreed upon during the foundations phase.

DSDM Phases and Products

The DSDM agile project framework describes a set of products that should be addressed as the project progresses (Figure 1.2). These items represent the solution itself (the project's major deliverable), as well as anything developed to aid in the evolution process and anything required to assist with project governance and control.

Not all goods are necessary for every project, and the formality associated with each product varies by project and company. Contractual agreements, business standards, and governance demands all have an impact on product formality.

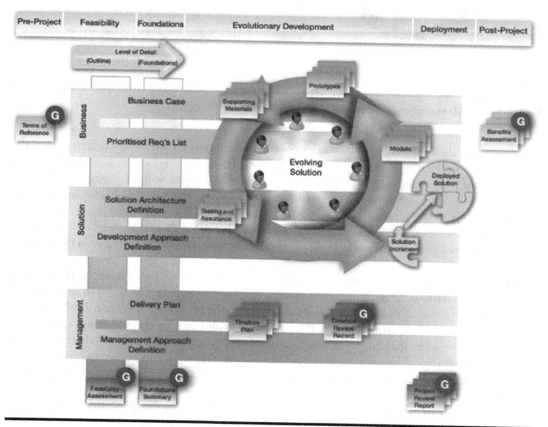

Figure 1.2   DSDM products and phases.

The figure above depicts the products and how they fit within the project lifecycle. Orange items are business-focused, green products contribute to the project's solution, and blue products address project management/control concerns.

Several of the products – those designated with G – may also play a role in governance procedures such as approval gateways, and they may be used to demonstrate the solution's compliance with corporate and regulatory standards as necessary.

DSDM Products

Terms of reference: The terms of reference provide a high-level explanation of the project's overall business rationale and top-level objectives. The fundamental purpose of the terms of reference is to define and justify the feasibility phase. It is classified as a governance tool because it may be used to prioritise projects within a portfolio.

Business case: The business case presents a vision and explanation for the project from a business standpoint. The business vision defines how the business will change over time and at the end of the project. The justification for the project is often based on an investment evaluation that determines whether the value of the solution to be supplied by the project is worth the cost of producing, supporting, and maintaining it in the future, all while maintaining an acceptable degree of risk. Baselines for the business case are normally generated as an outline at the end of feasibility, followed by a basis for development clearance at the end of foundations. It is formally reviewed at the end of each project increment to see if additional work is necessary.

Prioritised requirement list (PRL): The PRL specifies at a high level the requirements that the project must address and their priority in terms of satisfying the project's objectives and the needs of the company. Consideration of requirements begins in feasibility, and a baseline of the PRL specifies the project's scope at the end of foundations. Following that, depth will automatically adjust as detail emerges. Changes to the breadth (adding, deleting, or drastically changing high-level requirements) must be formalised in order to assure continuing alignment with the project's corporate strategy and maintain scope management.

The solution architecture definition establishes a high-level design framework for the solution. It is meant to encompass both the commercial and technical components of the solution in sufficient detail to clarify the solution's scope while allowing for evolutionary development.

Development approach definition: The development approach definition provides a high-level definition of the tools, processes, cultures, practices, and standards that will be used to evolve the solution. Importantly, it outlines how the solution's quality will be ensured. As a result, the definition describes a major component of the development approach: a testing and review process.

The delivery plan includes a high-level schedule of project increments as well as, at least for the first/imminent increment, the timeboxes that comprise that increment. It rarely addresses task-level detail unless tasks are being completed by individuals who are not members of the solution development team or before the solution development team is created.

Management approach definition: The management approach definition reflects the overall approach to project management and takes into account, from a management standpoint, how the project will be organised and planned, how stakeholders will be engaged in the project, and how progress will be demonstrated and, if necessary, reported. The product is specified in feasibility and baselined at the end of foundations; it will only evolve beyond that if circumstances change or if an assessment of the methodology uncovers areas for improvement.

Feasibility assessment: The feasibility assessment is a snapshot of the evolving company, solution, and management products outlined above at the end of the feasibility stage. Each of the products should be mature enough to contribute meaningfully to the judgement of whether the project is feasible or not. The feasibility assessment can be expressed as a baselined collection of items or as an executive summary that highlights the essential characteristics of each.

Foundations summary: The foundations summary depicts the emerging business, solution, and management products outlined above as they exist at the conclusion of the foundations phase. Each of the products should be developed enough to make an informed assessment about whether the project is likely to produce the requisite return on investment. Foundations summary can be expressed as a baselined collection of the goods listed above, or as an executive summary that highlights the important characteristics of each.

Evolving solution: The evolving solution consists of all appropriate components of the ultimate solution, as well as any intermediate deliverables required to investigate the specifics of the requirements and solution under design. At any given time, such components could be complete, a baseline for a partial solution (a solution increment), or a work in progress. Models, prototypes, supporting materials, and testing and review artefacts are all valuable. At the end of each project increment, the solution increment is put into production and becomes the deployed solution.

The timebox plan goes into detail about each timebox indicated in the delivery plan. It elaborates on the objectives specified for that timebox and describes the deliverables, as well as the actions required to achieve those deliverables and the resources required to complete the activity. The solution development team creates the timebox plan, which is frequently represented on a team board as work to be done, in progress, or completed. It is updated at least once a day at the daily stand-ups.

The timebox review record collects feedback from each review that occurs throughout a timebox. It explains what has been accomplished thus far, as well as any feedback that may have an impact on future plans. Where applicable, such as in a regulated setting, a formal, auditable record of review comments from experienced business advisors and other roles qualifies this as a governance solution.

The project review report is normally a single document that is incrementally updated at the conclusion of each project increment by adding new parts that are specific to that increment. At the end of each project increment, the aim of this product is to record input from the review of the supplied solution and confirm what has been delivered and what has not. (1) To capture learning points from the increment's retrospective focused on the process, practices, and contributing roles and responsibilities. (2) Where applicable, outline the business benefits that should now flow through the right use of the solution produced by the project up to this point. Following the final project increment, as part of project closure, a retrospective spanning the entire project is conducted, with the records for each project increment serving as partial input.

The benefits assessment illustrates how the benefits have accrued after a period of active operation. For projects where the benefits outlined in the business case are expected to accrue over time, a number of benefits assessments may be created on a periodic basis in accordance with the timescale used to justify the expenditure.

Summary: The items listed above provide guidance for the information required to promote good communication within a project. They are not required, and may not always be presented as documents. However, in situations where good governance and/or verification of standard compliance are critical, generating formal papers is preferable to just gaining a shared understanding. Although it may not be visible, documentation developed throughout the development phase and/or linked to the project's proactive management is likely to provide the most effective and robust audit trail if one is required.

It is also vital to note that DSDM products are only developed if they bring value to the project and/or the solution it produces. The most important element is that the project's stakeholders and participants understand what is required and what is being provided, and that quality is guaranteed. If documents truly help achieve this, generate them; otherwise, don't squander valuable time and effort doing so.

Roles and Responsibilities Within a DSDM Project

Any successful project is built on the foundation of effective teamwork. DSDM understands this and gives specific roles and responsibilities to each project team member, representing the business, solution/technical, management, and process interests. Everyone participating in a DSDM project works closely together to overcome potential communication hurdles (Figure 1.3).

The finest solutions come from self-organising, empowered teams. However, these teams and the individuals within them must actively accept responsibility for their empowerment within the agreed-upon limitations.

Role Categories

Project-level roles. The project-level responsibilities include business sponsor, business visionary, technical coordinator, project manager, and business analyst. They serve as project directors, managers, and coordinators as needed. They may be members of a project board or steering committee, with collective authority to direct the project. They are in charge of the project's governance, which includes liaising with external governance bodies as needed.

All project-level roles must adopt the facilitative, empowering leadership style that allows agile teams to learn as they go, achieving their goals on their own terms within an agreed-upon framework of empowerment.

Solution development team roles. The solution development team's positions include business ambassador, solution developer, solution tester, business analyst, and team leader. These are the project's "engine room" jobs. They shape and design the solution, and they are jointly accountable for its day-to-day development and commercial suitability. There may be one or more solution development teams in a project. Each team shall incorporate and cover all solution development team tasks and responsibilities.

Supporting roles. The supporting roles (business advisors, technical advisors, workshop facilitator, and DSDM Coach) provide project assistance and guidance on an as-needed basis throughout the lifecycle. The advisor roles may be performed by one or more subject matter experts, as needed.

The Roles Are

Business sponsor: This is the most senior project-level business position. The business sponsor is the project's champion, fully dedicated to the project, the proposed solution, and the delivery strategy. The business sponsor is solely accountable for the business case and project budget throughout (whether formally or informally articulated). The business sponsor must

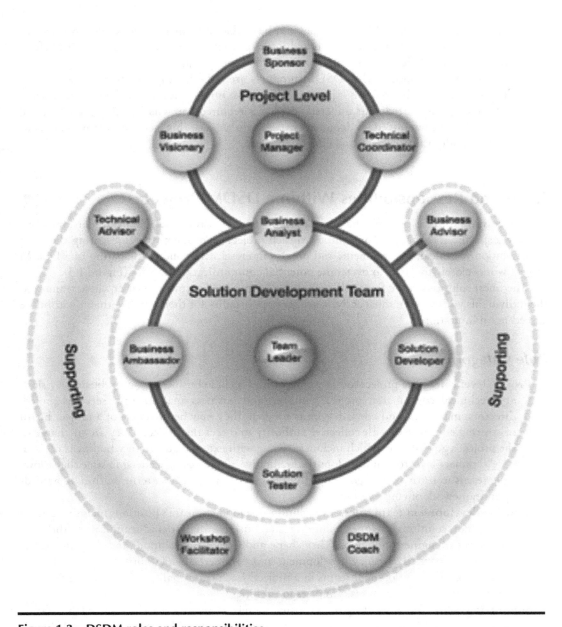

Figure 1.3 DSDM roles and responsibilities.

be in a high enough position within the firm to be able to address business concerns and make financial decisions.

Business visionary: This is a senior project-level business role that should be filled by a single person, as a project requires a single clear vision to minimise confusion and misdirection. The business visionary is more actively involved than the business sponsor and is in charge of interpreting the business sponsor's needs, expressing them to the team, and, when needed, ensuring they are appropriately represented in the business case. The business visionary remains involved throughout the project, providing strategic guidance to the team and ensuring that the delivered solution achieves the benefits indicated in the business case.

The technical coordinator is the project's technical authority, ensuring that the solution/technical roles work consistently, that the project is technically coherent, and that the intended technical standards are met. This function serves as the glue that connects the technical components of the project together, advising on technical decisions and innovation. The technical coordinator has the same technical responsibilities as the business visionary.

Project manager: In addition to providing high-level, agile-style leadership to the solution development team, this position is responsible for managing the working environment in which the solution is emerging. The project manager manages all aspects of project management at a high level; but, in accordance with the DSDM idea of empowerment, the project manager is required to delegate detailed planning of the actual delivery of the product(s) to members of the solution development team. Managing an empowered team necessitates a facilitative approach rather than a "command and control" strategy. The project manager is typically in charge of the project from start to finish. This role must involve both the business and technical components of project delivery, from foundations (if not feasibility) to deployment.

Business analyst: The business analyst actively supports the project-level functions while also being completely integrated into the solution development team. The business analyst fosters the link between the business and technical responsibilities, ensuring that accurate and suitable decisions are made on an ongoing basis regarding the evolving solution. The business analyst ensures that all solution development team members thoroughly assess and understand the business needs. The active participation of business users in the evolution of the solution is critical to the success of a DSDM project. As a result, it is critical that the business analyst does not serve as a mediator between solution development team members but rather supports and enables their collaboration.

The team leader ideally serves as a servant-leader for the solution development team, ensuring that it functions as a whole and achieves its goals. The team leader collaborates with the team to plan and coordinate all areas of product delivery on a comprehensive level. This is a leadership function rather than a management role, and the person in charge will ideally be chosen by his or her colleagues as the best individual to guide them through a certain stage of the project. In addition to their team leadership responsibilities, they are likely to take on another solution development team function (e.g., business analyst, business ambassador, solution developer, or solution tester).

The business ambassador is the primary representation of the company inside the solution development team. During foundations, the business ambassador has a considerable impact on the formulation and prioritisation of requirements. Once the requirements have been agreed upon and baselined (by the end of foundations), the business ambassador will offer day-to-day details on the needs during timeboxed development. This is either based on their own knowledge and experience, or on the expertise of business advisors. During the project's evolutionary development phase, the firm ambassador makes the primary decisions on behalf of the firm. As a result, the business ambassador must be someone who is valued by their business peers and has enough seniority, empowerment, and credibility to make judgements on behalf of the company in terms of ensuring the evolving solution is suitable for business use.

Solution developer: The solution developer works with the other solution development team roles to interpret business requirements and transform them into a solution increment that meets the functional and non-functional demands of the entire business.

Solution tester: The solution tester is an empowered solution development team role that performs testing throughout the project in accordance with the agreed-upon strategy.

Business advisor: Often a peer of the business ambassador, the business advisor is called upon to provide specialised, and often specialised, input to solution development or testing – a business subject matter expert. The business advisor may be a solution's intended user or benefactor, or they may provide legal or regulatory advice with which the solution must comply.

Technical advisor: The technical advisor assists the team by offering specialised, and often specialised, technical advice to the project, typically from the perspective of people in charge of operational change management, operational support, solution maintenance, and so on.

Workshop facilitator: The workshop facilitator is in charge of planning, arranging, and facilitating workshops to guarantee that a group of people work together to achieve a certain goal in a limited amount of time. The workshop facilitator should be independent of the workshop's outcome.

DSDM Coach: When a team has minimal experience with DSDM, the job of the DSDM Coach is critical in assisting team members to get the most out of the method while remaining within the context and limits of the larger organisation in which they work.

Summary

DSDM recognises roles in two dimensions: categories and interests.
 Roles are divided into **three categories**:

- **Project-level roles** include business sponsor, business visionary, technical coordinator, project manager, and business analyst (also part of the solution development team).
- **Solution development team roles** include business ambassador, solution developer, solution tester, team leader, and business analyst (project-level role).
- **Supporting roles** include business advisor, technical advisor, workshop facilitator, and DSDM Coach.

And four interests:

- **Business interests** are addressed by the business sponsor, business visionary, business ambassador, and business advisor roles.
- Roles such as technical coordinator, solution developer, solution tester, and technical advisor address **technical interests**.
- **Management interests** – covered by the project manager and team leader responsibilities.
- **Process interests** are addressed by the workshop facilitator and DSDM Coach roles.

The business analyst position involves both business and solution/technical interests.

Chapter 2

Introduction to Agile Project Management

The Agile Manifesto and Core Values

Agile Manifesto and Core Values

In 2001, seventeen thought leaders in software development formed the Agile Alliance and drafted the Agile Manifesto. This document describes the fundamental idea that underpins agile development approaches, which prioritise flexibility, collaboration, and providing workable solutions above strict planning.

The **Agile Manifesto** asserts the following:

- Individuals and interactions versus processes and tools.
- Working software above detailed documentation.
- Customer collaboration versus contract negotiation.
- Responding to change rather than following a plan

Core Values of Agile

The following four assertions explain the core values that underlie agile approaches:

a. **Prioritising people**: While processes and technologies are important, agile recognises that successful projects rely on the talent, communication, and collaboration of those involved.
b. **Delivering value**: Rather than lengthy documentation cycles, agile emphasises developing functioning versions of the solution early and frequently. This enables input and guarantees that the final product fits the users' needs.
c. **Embracing collaboration**: Agile promotes collaboration between the development team and customers or stakeholders. This active cooperation results in improved designs and solutions for real-world challenges.

DOI: 10.4324/9781032688435-3

d. **Adapting to change**: Agile recognises that requirements evolve and unexpected changes occur. Projects should be designed to adjust to change and learn during the development process, rather than adhering to the initial plan at all costs.

Let me provide you with a few real-world examples of organisations that have implemented these core values:

Prioritising individuals

a. Intermountain Healthcare (hospital system) uses agile techniques in areas such as clinical decision support system development. This requires tight collaboration among physicians, IT specialists, and project managers to ensure that solutions really assist clinician workflow.
b. Nurse-led innovation: Often, nurses have firsthand knowledge of wasteful processes. An agile attitude encourages hospitals to host hackathons or other similar programmes, allowing nurses to exchange challenges and collaborate on solutions.

Delivering value

a. Babylon Health (AI for healthcare): Their rapid development of symptom checkers and telehealth services exemplifies an agile methodology. Instead of spending years refining one platform, they focus on releasing viable versions fast to meet patient needs and then iteratively improving.
b. Pilot projects: Hospitals may use agile concepts to roll out innovative care models in a specialised unit initially. This emphasis on a "minimum viable product" allows for course correction before expanding throughout the hospital.

Embracing collaboration

a. Roche Pharmaceuticals: Their use of agile in drug development involves improved collaboration among researchers, data scientists, and regulatory teams. This shared ownership of the project helps to expedite the process and accelerate knowledge sharing.
b. Patient advocacy groups: Including them in initiatives involving app development or patient education materials is an excellent example of agile collaboration. They provide distinct views to verify that solutions truly satisfy the requirements of persons impacted by certain diseases.

Adapting to change

a. COVID-19 response: Hospitals that showed agility during the pandemic had to re-prioritise projects on the fly. Agile thinking enabled the rapid installation of telehealth and the repurposing of venues to fulfil emergency requirements.
b. Evolving treatment protocols: Cancer centres may use agile-like systems to frequently update care pathways based on the most recent findings. This emphasis on responsiveness encourages patients to receive the most current treatments possible.

The Agile Mindset

The Agile Manifesto and its values signify a change in thinking. This is about:

   a. **Empiricism** is the practice of learning by doing and making course adjustments depending on real-world findings.
   b. **Transparency** entails open communication regarding progress, difficulties, and comments.
   c. **Empowerment** entails granting teams the trust and authority to adapt and find the best solutions.

Examples of agile mindset

- Chief Information Officers (CIOs) in agile hospitals: People in this position frequently promote agile-like approaches. They understand that while healthcare requires rigour, it also requires flexibility to respond rapidly to changes in the healthcare industry.
- While the Food and Drug Administration (FDA) is a regulatory organisation, its increased willingness to approve medical devices using iterative development models demonstrates an appreciation of the importance of flexibility balanced with safety.

Agile in Healthcare

Agile's values are perfectly aligned with the requirements of healthcare initiatives. Its emphasis on collaboration strengthens multidisciplinary healthcare teams. The agility helps negotiate regulatory changes, and the emphasis on producing value keeps patient outcomes in mind.

Popular Agile Frameworks (Scrum, Kanban, XP, etc.) With a Brief Overview of Each

The Agile Manifesto serves as the driving principle, while frameworks give more organised techniques for implementing agile values in real-world projects. Let's take a quick look at some of the most popular:

1. **Scrum**

   Scrum emphasises iterative development and the rapid delivery of working solutions. Projects are divided into brief "sprints" (usually 1–4 weeks) with specified objectives.

   Team structure: Scrum teams are cross-functional and self-managing, with a product owner (representing the customer), a scrum master (facilitator), and developers.

   Key practices: Sprint planning, daily standup meetings (daily scrums), sprint reviews, and retrospectives to evaluate and improve the process (Figure 2.1).

2. **Kanban**

   Kanban focuses on visualising work, minimising work in progress (WIP), and improving workflow efficiency. It uses a kanban board to visualise work at various levels, such as "To Do," "In Progress," and "Done."

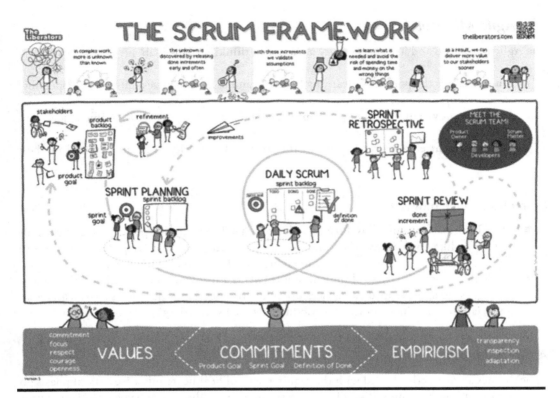

Figure 2.1   The scrum framework.

Kanban is more flexible than scrum in terms of timeboxing and roles. It can be simply implemented by current teams without requiring significant restructuring.

Key practices: Continuous flow of work, WIP limits to eliminate bottlenecks, and an emphasis on analysing workflow metrics to discover opportunities for improvement.

3. **Extreme Programming (XP)**

Focus: XP is designed for software development, emphasising technical quality and adaptability to changing requirements.

Key practices include pair programming, test-driven development, frequent releases, and continuous integration.

XP is most suited for contexts with unknown or changing needs, as well as teams with strong engineering procedures.

Other Agile Frameworks

The Scaled Agile Framework (SAFe) offers direction for applying agile methods to big projects and companies.

Crystal is a family of agile techniques with varied levels of structure to match the complexity of the project.

Lean development: Applying lean manufacturing techniques to software development, with a focus on reducing waste and increasing value.

Choosing the Right Framework

The optimal agile framework for a healthcare project is based on aspects such as

Project size and complexity: Scrum or kanban is a good starting point, but large projects may benefit from systems such as SAFe.

Team culture: Self-organising teams may benefit from scrum, but existing teams may find kanban's progressive deployment easier.

Nature of the project: XP is well-suited to software development, but kanban's adaptive approach may be useful for more general projects involving process improvement.

Key Agile Practices (Iterations, Sprints, User Stories, Retrospectives)

Scrum, kanban, and other agile frameworks use specific methods to put the agile Manifesto's ideals into action. Here are some of the key elements that form the agile approach to project management:

1. **Iterations and sprints**

    Breaking work down: Agile initiatives believe that requirements and solutions develop. Instead of a single major deliverable at the end, work is divided into smaller, iterative phases.

    Sprints: In scrum, these iterations are referred to as sprints – short, time-boxed periods (often 1–4 weeks) in which a specific amount of work is completed.

    Iterations provide early feedback, course correction if needed, and help offer value to consumers faster.

2. **User stories**

    Customer-focused requirements: User stories are brief explanations of a feature or functionality from the user's perspective. They take the following format: "As a [type of user], I want to [action], so that [benefit]."

    Why do user stories help? They focus on what the solution has to achieve for the end user, rather than just technical specs. This encourages ideas that truly meet real-world demands.

3. **Daily standups (or scrums)**

    Quick coordination: These are short (15-minute) concentrated sessions held every day during a sprint. Each team member presents what they accomplished the previous day, what they intend to work on, and any obstacles.

    Standups increase transparency, identify potential barriers early on, and encourage team collaboration.

4. **Sprint reviews**

    Demonstrating value: At the end of each sprint, stakeholders are shown a functioning increment of the solution. This isn't a polished product, but it's useful enough to generate feedback.

    Benefits: Regular evaluations maintain alignment with user needs, allow for course correction, and foster confidence among stakeholders as they observe progress iteratively.

5. **Retrospective**

    Continuous improvement: Following each sprint (or iteration), the team evaluates what went well, what could be improved, and develops action plans for the next one.

    Benefits: Retrospectives promote an environment of learning and adaptability. They enable teams to optimise their processes, which improves efficiency and morale.

Agile Practices in Healthcare

These practices work well for healthcare projects:

a. Instead of technical language, a project might include stories like: "As a nurse, I want to view a patient's lab results directly in their chart, so that I can make informed care decisions."
b. Quick feedback loops: Iterative development is essential when creating care pathways or decision-support technologies. These methods enable refinement based on how the tools are utilised in real-world scenarios.

Chapter 3

DSDM and Agile: Synergies and Differences

How DSDM and Agile Address the Specific Needs of Healthcare Projects

While both are based on the agile ideology, DSDM provides a structured framework designed for larger projects, whereas agile methodologies such as scrum, kanban, and XP give a variety of ways for specific needs. Together, they form an effective instrument for healthcare project management. Here's how they relate to healthcare's challenges: Let me also provide scenarios to illustrate.

Adapting to Change

Healthcare reality: Regulatory changes, new treatment procedures, and public health crises necessitate flexibility.

DSDM and Agile Solutions: The iterative, feedback-driven nature of DSDM and agile is compatible with this setting. Projects might view change as a learning opportunity rather than a danger to the initial strategy.

Scenario: As a hospital is installing a new EHR system, a federal rule change affects how pharmaceutical data must be recorded.

DSDM/agile approach: Iterations and feedback loops avoid large reworks in the end. Teams can gradually modify the EHR data structure and reporting modules in response to the regulatory adjustment.

Prioritising Patient Outcomes

Healthcare reality: Project success cannot be determined only by job accomplishment. The ultimate goal is to improve patient care and well-being.

DSDM and Agile Solutions: The emphasis on "fitness for business purpose" (DSDM) and delivering working solutions (agile) prioritises patient impact. User stories and frequent reviews guarantee that solutions fit the problems they are intended to solve.

DOI: 10.4324/9781032688435-4

Scenario: A project is underway to create a patient education portal geared on diabetes care.

DSDM/agile approach: Rather than a comprehensive launch after months of work, they prioritise developing a core part (e.g., on food and exercise). User feedback on that area would actively impact the creation of the following modules, ensuring that the end result is truly useful.

Empowering Collaboration

Healthcare reality: Solutions must be suitable for clinicians, IT teams, administrators, and patients. Siloed work leads to low adoption and efficiency.

DSDM and Agile Solutions: Cross-functional teams are key to DSDM, and collaboration is an important agile value. This promotes different perspectives, improved problem-solving, and solutions that benefit everyone involved.

Scenario: Changing a hospital's triage procedure affects ER doctors, nurses, and admissions staff.

DSDM/agile approach: The DSDM framework ensures that all groups are represented. Kanban might visually represent the workflow, allowing all stakeholders to engage with improvement suggestions.

Managing Risks and Ensuring Compliance

Healthcare reality: Patient safety and data privacy are critical. Regulatory compliance can be difficult and evolve over time.

DSDM and Agile Solutions: Risk management and control are fundamental DSDM principles. Agile's iterations make it easier to identify concerns early on and continuously assess compliance.

Scenario: Create software for remote monitoring of patients with chronic diseases.

DSDM/agile approach: DSDM emphasises "demonstrate control," but agile's iterations enable regular security and compliance testing. Issues such as data encryption are addressed throughout, rather than as an afterthought.

Navigating the Human Element

Healthcare reality: Success is frequently dependent on the adaptability and buy-in of healthcare workers. Solutions that affect their process encounter an additional layer of complication.

DSDM and Agile Solutions: Agile principles assist in designing solutions with users, rather than for them, by actively involving clinicians from the outset. This fosters better adoption and reduces unexpected workflow disruptions.

Scenario: Implementing a new medication management system for nurses.

DSDM/agile approach: Nurses are involved from the start, sharing insights into their workflow via user stories. Frequent demos and training on the new system, based on feedback from iterations, facilitate the transfer and promote adoption.

Healthcare settings: These examples could be applied in hospitals, pharmaceutical businesses, or public health organisations, demonstrating DSDM/agile's broad applicability.

Not every method is perfect; there are still issues. Agile techniques necessitate a certain amount of support from healthcare professionals, which can be difficult to obtain at times.

Success in healthcare projects requires more than just technical expertise. DSDM and agile frameworks are ideally suited to the dynamic, collaborative, and values-driven nature of the healthcare industry.

Areas Where DSDM and Agile Approaches Complement Each Other

While there are differences between DSDM and agile methodologies such as scrum or kanban, they share a core philosophy and make an effective combination for healthcare project success. Here are some key areas where they complement each other:

Structured flexibility: DSDM provides a predefined framework with stages and roles, whereas agile techniques give flexibility within that framework. This is useful in healthcare settings when a combination of predictability and adaptability is required.

Big picture and iterations: DSDM excels at outlining the overall project vision, ensuring that it aligns with the organisation's objectives. Agile frameworks such as scrum excel at breaking down work into manageable iterations and delivering results progressively.

Stakeholder collaboration: DSDM actively engages stakeholders throughout its life cycle. Agile focuses on regular communication and feedback loops. This combination approach guarantees that all viewpoints are examined, resulting in solutions that actually fulfil the demands of healthcare professionals, patients, and the organisation.

Risk management: The DSDM's emphasis on "demonstrate control" encourages proactive risk identification and mitigation. Agile approaches enable early discovery of potential problems and fast course correction, which improves risk management throughout the project.

Scalability: DSDM provides structure for larger or more complicated healthcare initiatives, which may require more control than single-team scrum. However, agile approaches can be used to optimise execution inside the DSDM phases.

How does this synergy look in practice. Let me provide you with some examples:

Example 1: Developing Clinical Decision Support (CDS) Software

The challenge: Ensuring that the tool is evidence-based, fits within physician workflows, and meets regulatory standards.

The DSDM framework describes the project's scope, high-level timelines, key stakeholder groups (clinicians, IT, regulators), and risk assessments.

Agile execution: Iterative development takes place within the phases of DSDM. Scrum sprints could focus on developing specific CDS modules (e.g., medication interaction alerts). Clinicians provide input on clinical accuracy and ease of use during regular demonstrations.

Example 2: Redesigning the Hospital Discharge Process

The challenge: Enhance patient outcomes, decrease readmissions, and optimise resource utilisation. This includes clinicians, social workers, and possibly external care providers.

DSDM framework establishes an overarching project framework, establishes success measures, and provides a comprehensive approach that takes into account all stakeholders.

Agile execution: Kanban might visualise the present process and identify bottlenecks. Frequent reviews allow for speedy testing of changes (e.g., new patient education materials) and assessment of their influence on readmission rates.

Example 3: Pharmaceutical Drug Development

The challenge: Strict restrictions, long development cycles, and the possibility of research discoveries altering the course.

DSDM framework structures the project into phases that correspond to regulatory milestones. Iterative development at each step enables adjustments based on study findings. This could affect the drug's formulation or target indications.

Agile execution: Scrum sprints might concentrate on certain trial stages or data analysis tasks. This attention enables rapid adaptation to new knowledge or problems.

Real-World Considerations

Healthcare innovation centres: Within major hospitals, innovation centres frequently use DSDM-style methodologies with agile execution. This allows for broader strategic goals while maintaining flexibility in the development process.

Digital health startups: When resources are limited, DSDM prioritisation mixed with agile's "minimum viable product" focus is effective. Consider apps for patient symptom tracking or medication adherence.

Public health agencies: DSDM can help build a multi-pronged programme (e.g., tackling vaccination hesitancy), whereas agile iterations enable for quick changes to messaging or outreach approaches based on the target audience's response.

Comparing and Contrasting the Two Methodologies for Effective Decision-Making

While both DSDM and agile encourage flexibility and collaboration, there are differences in how they guide decision-making throughout a healthcare project (Table 3.1).

Table 3.1   Methodology Differences

Feature	DSDM	Agile Methods (Scrum, Kanban, etc.)
Decision-making style	Structured and collaborative	More decentralised and team-focused
Focus	Fitness for business purpose throughout	Prioritising value delivery in iterations
Roles	Clear decision points for key stakeholders	Teams make many day-to-day decisions
Emphasis	Risk management and proactive control	Embracing change and rapid adaptation
Change management	Accommodates change within a framework	Built around continuous iterations

How This Affects Projects

DSDM

Well-suited for: Large-scale decisions requiring strategic alignment.

Decision-making process: At the end of each DSDM phase, structured reviews are conducted with specified stakeholders and business sponsors.

Agile

Well-suited for: Iteration-level decisions (e.g., which features to prioritise in the next sprint, changing a procedure based on early testing).

Decision-making process: Empowers a cross-functional team. Scrum masters facilitate, but daily standups and retrospectives stimulate collaborative feedback.

Real-world scenario: Implementation of a new telehealth platform

Background: A mid-sized hospital system is starting telehealth to improve patient access to care. This includes selecting a platform, providing clinician training, integrating with current systems, and managing change throughout the organisation.

DSDM in Action

Feasibility and foundations: Key stakeholders (clinicians, administrators, IT, and possibly patient representatives) evaluate solutions. Decisions: Video or audio-only? Cloud-based or in-house servers? What level of integration with the EHR? These affect cost, security, and long-term objectives. DSDM alignment ensures that decisions support the overall picture of care delivery.

Evolutionary development: Even after choosing a platform, DSDM's iterative approach influences rollout decisions. Will they start with pilot programmes in specific departments? Does the entire EHR integration occur at once or in stages?

Agile in Action

Selecting the core platform: While DSDM provides the foundation, agile methodologies can be employed for evaluation. Short platform demos with user feedback. Teams evaluate platforms iteratively, which helps inform their selection.

Features and interfaces: Once the fundamental infrastructure is in place, scrum sprints may focus on developing specific features. Decisions: Does the video quality require improvement? Can appointment scheduling be simplified? These are driven by daily standup meetings and sprint reviews.

Change management: Agile's emphasis on feedback influences how they handle clinician training. Early users provide feedback on the training programme and indicate interface issues. This enables changes during the rollout.

Where DSDM and Agile Meet

Major obstacles: If there is a significant regulatory change affecting patient privacy during video visits, the project may be paused. This larger realignment decision is likely the result of a DSDM-level analysis.

Unexpected success: If demand exceeds expectations, DSDM stakeholders will most likely be involved in a rapid scaling decision (additional licences, faster hiring of support people).

Additional Considerations

Hospital size: A simple clinic may not have the complex stakeholder structure suggested by DSDM. Agile alone may be adequate for a minor telehealth installation.

Vendor involvement: If the platform vendor is substantially involved, their methodology (which may be agile) will be compatible with the hospital's procedure.

Effective Use: Combining Strengths

The key to success depends on understanding where each methodology excels and consciously blending them:

DSDM: The Strategic Backbone

Overall alignment: DSDM focuses on the "why" of the project, ensuring that it supports the healthcare organisation's mission, long-term goals, and meets a true need.

Structure for complexity: The DSDM provides a framework for managing diverse projects. This is useful when the stakeholders are diverse (patients, regulators, etc.) and decisions have far-reaching consequences for the organisation.

Risk mitigation: The emphasis on control in DSDM encourages early identification of risks (regulatory, financial). This is not about avoiding risk, but about managing it in a disciplined manner.

Agile: The Execution Engine

Adaptability to the unpredictable: Agile's iterative approach implies that change will occur. This is consistent with healthcare, where new standards or treatment choices may arise even mid-project.

Focus on usable value: Agile avoids getting bogged down in the flawless plan. Instead, it focuses on producing working chunks that stakeholders can use and provide feedback on.

Team empowerment: Cross-functional agile teams with decision-making autonomy can address challenges effectively. This is especially essential for workflow concerns that clinicians or frontline personnel encounter personally.

How It Works Together (Beyond the Telehealth Example)

New treatment guidelines: New, game-changing guidelines are published midway through a project aimed at building care pathways. DSDM's structure supports a review: Do they halt and reflect? Do they modularise the paths, allowing for updates?

Headaches associated with EHR upgrades: Even with a DSDM-like plan, the update is a mess. Agile approaches enable teams to quickly troubleshoot workarounds rather than bringing everything to a halt while waiting for a great solution.

Public health crisis: DSDM may give an overall response strategy (outreach and vaccination sites). However, the flexibility of agile to react to changing conditions on the ground would enhance day-to-day testing, communication, and so on.

Caution: It is not one-size-fits-all.
The ideal balance will differ between projects:

■ Small-scale, well-defined project: Agile alone may be sufficient (creating an informational brochure for a specific condition).
■ Highly regulated, long-term project: DSDM structure may be more important.

IMPLEMENTING DSDM AND AGILE IN HEALTHCARE PROJECTS

Chapter 4

Preparing for Agile Healthcare Projects

Assessing Organisational Readiness for DSDM and Agile

Successful adoption of DSDM and agile does not occur in a vacuum. Assessing your healthcare organisation's readiness provides a solid foundation for a successful transition. Key aspects to evaluate are:

Organisational Culture

Adaptability: Is the organisation used to change, or is there a strong tendency for sticking to pre-determined plans? Agile thrives in environments that are open to changing course.

Here are a few example questions:

Our organisation is comfortable changing directions mid-project if necessary.

We are open to experimenting with new ways of working, even if there's a risk of initial setbacks.

When a plan needs to change, teams are able to adjust quickly and effectively.

Collaboration: Are teams usually siloed? DSDM and agile prioritise breaking down barriers. A culture of cross-functional collaboration and shared ownership of project achievements is essential.

Here are a few example questions:

Teams from different departments (e.g., clinical, IT, administration) frequently work together on projects.

I feel comfortable sharing my ideas and concerns with team members from other departments.

There's a sense of shared responsibility for project outcomes, regardless of departmental roles.

DOI: 10.4324/9781032688435-6

Mindset: Does the organisation place equal weight on learning from setbacks and successes? Agile values iteration, which includes the risk that some first solutions will be imperfect.

Here are a few example questions:

We view setbacks as opportunities for learning and improvement.

We celebrate the process of continuous improvement rather than only focusing on the final product.

Taking calculated risks to find better solutions is encouraged.

Tips for Phrasing Questions

Avoid asking leading questions. Don't frame things as if there's a "right" solution (e.g., "We SHOULD be more adaptable").

Use straightforward language: Drop the jargon. Ensure that everyone understands, not just those who are already familiar with agile.

A mix of positive and negative: Having some statements where "disagreeing" is a sign of preparation prevents individuals from agreeing on everything.

Additional considerations:

Include "Not Applicable": Some questions may be unrelated to specific roles in your organisation.

Balance using open-ended questions: Allow comments such as "My biggest concern about Agile is…" to gain qualitative insights.

Leadership Support

Understanding and buy-in: Do senior executives recognise the benefits of DSDM and agile beyond mere buzzwords? Their enthusiastic support signifies a transformation within the organisation.

Here are a few example questions:

Our senior leaders can clearly explain the benefits of DSDM/Agile approaches for our specific projects.

Leadership's support for Agile goes beyond just using the terminology.

Our leaders understand that Agile approaches might require changes to traditional project management processes.

Empowerment: Will leaders cede some decision-making authority to teams? Agile's team-centric strategy requires trust to be genuinely effective.

Here are a few example questions:

Leadership trusts project teams to make day-to-day decisions within the broader project goals.

I feel comfortable proposing changes to a project plan without multiple layers of approval.

Teams have the authority to adjust their approach based on feedback and results.

Champions: Identifying leaders (preferably both clinical and administrative) who support agile can help generate momentum and overcome objections.
Here are a few example questions:

There are visible leaders within the organisation who actively champion the use of Agile methods.
Leadership encourages staff to learn about and participate in Agile initiatives.
I know who to reach out to if I have questions or need support in implementing Agile approaches.

Additional tips:

Target the right audience: If possible, provide a version of the survey exclusively for leaders to evaluate their own self-assessments.
Consider framing some sentences, such "agree," to signal a potential problem area (e.g., "All major project decisions require multiple layers of leadership approval").

Resources and Training

Staffing: Can workers be assigned to a specific project, or will they be dragged into day-to-day operations? DSDM and agile require a continual team focus.
Here are a few example questions:

I have the time and availability to dedicate myself to a project team consistently.
Our organisation is able to protect project team members from being pulled into day-to-day operational tasks.
There's a process in place to backfill roles temporarily when individuals are dedicated to a project.

Training requirements: Do employees comprehend the ideas and "why" behind the shift? Training is more than simply tools; it is also about changing one's perspective and collaboration.
Here are a few example questions:

I have a good understanding of the core principles behind DSDM and Agile methodologies.
I have access to the necessary training and resources to learn about Agile tools and techniques.
Our organisation emphasises training on Agile collaboration skills, not just technical tools.

Budget: Agile does not always equal cheaper, but budgeting practices may need to change. As teams learn the new process, there may be a higher initial investment in the planning phases (under DSDM).

Here are a few example questions:

Our organisation is prepared to allocate the necessary budget for Agile adoption (training, tools, potential process changes).

I understand that Agile projects may have different budgeting needs than traditional projects.

There's flexibility in the budget to allow for adjustments based on learnings during the project.

Additional considerations:

Role-certain questions: Ask questions tailored to certain groups ("As a physician, I can realistically participate in regular team meetings").

Beyond initial training: As one-time training is insufficient, include a question such as "I feel there will be ongoing support for my agile learning journey."

Project Suitability

Complexity: Is the project large enough to support the DSDM framework, or is plain agile more appropriate? Small efforts might serve as an excellent trial ground for larger changes.

Here are a few example questions:

Our projects often have multiple stakeholders with differing needs.

The requirements for our projects tend to evolve over time.

Many of our projects involve multiple teams or departments working together.

Regulatory constraints: Are some areas of healthcare so heavily controlled that true flexibility is impossible? It's preferable to be realistic about where DSDM/agile can provide the most value.

Here are a few example questions:

The regulatory requirements for our projects allow for flexibility in our development process.

We have processes in place to address changing regulations during a project's lifecycle.

There's room for iterative development and validation within our regulatory compliance framework.

Urgency: If there is a truly urgent crisis, a command-and-control method may be unavoidable. Agile excels at complexity, not chaos.

Here are a few example questions:

Our projects frequently have tight deadlines with little room for adjustment.

Unexpected changes or roadblocks severely derail our projects.

We rarely have the luxury of delivering features incrementally, requiring a complete product launch all at once.

How to Interpret Answers

For these questions, it is great if responders can provide examples in addition to their assessment.

Search for:

Patterns: If most projects have tight timelines and strict standards, agile may be difficult to execute widely.

"Pockets of suitability": Even if organisation-wide agile adoption is unlikely, certain sorts of projects may be ideal candidates to test the approach.

Important note: Do not let these questions exist in a vacuum. Combine them with open-ended feedback to see how employees are currently handling complexity or tight deadlines. That might reveal some agile-like thinking that was previously present!

Key Takeaway

Readiness is a continuum, not a definitive checklist. Being open about your strengths and short-comings allows you to adjust your implementation plan, increasing the likelihood of long-term success.

Building a Cross-Functional Agile Team in Healthcare Settings

The emphasis on collaboration across various expertise is a key pillar of both DSDM and agile methodologies. In healthcare, this principle is critical for guaranteeing solutions that are really patient-centred and effective. Here's how to form a strong team:

Key Roles

Clinicians, including doctors, nurses, therapists, and chemists, share firsthand knowledge of patient needs, workflow realities, and the possible impact of the solution.

IT specialists include developers, data analysts, and individuals who understand the limitations and opportunities of existing healthcare systems (e.g., EHR).

Administrators are individuals who understand resource allocation, operational limits, and how the project fits into the organisation's goals.

Patient representatives (if applicable): Depending on the project, direct patient involvement ensures that solutions meet their specific needs and are built with accessibility in mind.

Project manager/scrum master: Helps to streamline team operations, maintain communication, and remove impediments.

Business sponsor: Represents the project's stakeholders and promotes its value to the organisation.

Team Formation Considerations

Availability: Can key persons devote sufficient time to the project? Agile demands consistency, not just occasional input.

Openness to collaboration: Look for individuals who are eager to learn from various fields and question their own assumptions.

Early career therapists may have new ideas, while seasoned personnel provide background. Blending experience levels encourages well-rounded thinking.

Empowerment: The team must feel that their contributions shape the solution. Agile is more than just having the appropriate people; it's also about giving them a voice.

Challenges and Solutions

Siloed mentality: Emphasise how each position contributes to the overarching aim of improving patient care. Use project-specific examples to emphasise this.

Scheduling conflicts: (particularly with clinicians) Plan ahead of time, hold short but focused sessions, and consider using asynchronous collaboration tools.

Technical jargon: Encourage plain-language explanations. Visual aids (whiteboards during meetings) help close knowledge gaps faster than technical material.

Agile in Healthcare: Team Dynamics

Daily standups: Keep them brief and focused on progress, impediments, and what each individual hopes to accomplish that day.

Demos and feedback: Share workable versions early, even if they are imperfect. Collect physician feedback to confirm that tools are genuinely usable in real-world settings.

Shared responsibility: The team celebrates achievements together and accepts common responsibility for disappointments. This fosters trust in addressing complex challenges jointly.

Remember that the membership of an ideal agile team will change depending on the unique healthcare project and the organisation's culture.

Let me provide you with a few scenarios to illustrate this theme.

Scenario 1: Redesigning an Emergency Department (ED) Workflow

The team includes an emergency room (ER) physician, an ER nurse, a charge nurse, a patient flow coordinator, an IT specialist familiar with the ED's tracking system, and a hospital administrator.

Why cross-functionality matters: Physicians and nurses can provide immediate insights into bottlenecks. IT knows data flow, whereas the administrator sees the budget picture. Together, they avoid methods that solve one problem while creating two more.

Example agile practices: Frequently demonstrated how modifications to the triage process are replicated in the software. The team immediately determines whether it speeds things up or makes things more confusing.

Scenario 2: Create a Patient Education App for Diabetes Management

The team includes an endocrinologist, a diabetes nurse educator, app developers, a UX designer, a patient advocate (preferably someone who has diabetes), and a project manager.

Why cross-functionality matters: Clinicians guarantee content accuracy, developers focus on technical execution, and the patient advocate ensures that it is understandable to the intended audience.

Example agile practices: Short sprints concentrate on essential features (blood sugar recording and medication reminders). The patient advocate tests constantly to avoid usability concerns that may alienate users.

Scenario 3: Public Health Campaign to Encourage Vaccination (During Flu Season, etc.)

The team includes public health authorities, communications specialists, data analysts, a community engagement coordinator, and representatives from the target population(s).

Why cross-functional matters: Data determines where to focus, but community representatives ensure that messaging is culturally appropriate and reaches the correct people. It must be not just accurate, but also trustworthy.

Example agile practices: Short repetitions of messaging (posters, social media). Early feedback loops with the community may suggest that a totally true message isn't convincing.

Additional Notes

Role fluidity: In small organisations, one individual may wear numerous hats (e.g., the IT guy may be the scrum master). Agile is adaptive in this situation.

External partners: A vendor developing a medical device could be a member of the team. Their development process will need to be compatible with the hospital's agile strategy.

Evolving teams: As projects evolve, the required expertise may alter. The initial focus on EHR integration necessitates extensive IT; subsequently, when the emphasis switches to user training, this requirement decreases.

Securing Stakeholder Buy-In and Overcoming Cultural Barriers

Successful implementation of DSDM and agile in healthcare necessitates gaining buy-in from a diverse collection of stakeholders and proactively overcoming potential cultural opposition. Here's how to tackle this:

Who Are Your Stakeholders?

- Executives and leaders have the authority to approve financing and initiate organisational-wide changes.
- Clinicians: Front-line staff whose workflows and processes are frequently impacted by agile projects.
- IT Department: Required collaborators in any project including a large technological component.
- Patients and carers: Depending on the project, ensuring their voices are heard is critical, especially for patient-facing solutions.
- Regulatory bodies (potentially): Understanding the needs and restrictions of projects that must adhere to rigorous rules is critical.

Strategies to Gain Buy-In

Focus on the "why": Highlight the specific pain areas that agile addresses (inefficient workflows, costly project delays, misalignment of solutions, and real-world healthcare demands).

Success stories: Share case studies (preferably from similar healthcare contexts) demonstrating the benefits of agile and DSDM. Hard data demonstrating improved patient outcomes or efficiency is convincing.

Don't overpromise: Agile isn't a miraculous solution. Be open about both the potential benefits and the necessity for the organisation to change how it manages projects.

Involve stakeholders early: Do not reveal a fully fledged agile plan. Gather feedback during the readiness assessment and team-building phases to develop a sense of co-ownership.

Champions and change agents: Identify enthusiastic leaders across departments to promote agile adoption and handle team issues.

Overcoming Cultural Barriers

Fear of change: Healthcare frequently emphasises predictability. Emphasise that agile allows for change inside a controlled framework, hence increasing adaptability.

"We've always done it this way": Explain how agile builds on the strengths of existing processes while tackling inefficiencies or outmoded approaches.

"No time for this": Show how agile's emphasis on delivering value quickly can reduce long-term effort rather than increase it.

Focus on documentation over results: Communicate that agile prioritises outputs and working solutions, and streamline paperwork wherever possible.

Key Points

Tailor your message: A CIO's concerns are not the same as those of a doctor. Discuss each stakeholder group's priorities.

Small wins: Try agile on an appropriate project. Success instils confidence and knocks down barriers to further deployment.

Training isn't enough. Mentorship and continuing assistance are essential, particularly for people new to agile methods of working.

Chapter 5

Project Initiation and Planning With DSDM

DSDM Feasibility and Foundations Phases for Healthcare Projects

Within the DSDM lifecycle, the feasibility and foundations phases lay the groundwork for educated decision-making, alignment with healthcare's particular issues, and a dedication to solutions that actually match stakeholder needs.

Feasibility Phase

Purpose: Determine whether the project is in line with the organisation's goals, technically feasible, and likely to deliver value. In healthcare, this includes regulatory limits and possibly ethical concerns.

Key questions in healthcare:

Is there a legitimate clinical need? Long-term adoption depends on addressing a provider pain point or enhancing treatment quality.

Are the technological needs realistic? Does the existing infrastructure support it? Are there any data integration issues with EHRs and other systems?

Can we navigate the regulatory landscape? Understanding data privacy, safety reporting, and other compliance obligations from the start saves time and money later.

Is this the perfect time? Is this consistent with other organisational aims, or are resources already stretched?

Foundations Phase

The purpose is to define the project's scope, outline high-level requirements, identify hazards, and develop the initial project plan. Here is where DSDM's emphasis on "fitness for business purpose" shines.

DOI: 10.4324/9781032688435-7

Key activities in healthcare:

In-depth stakeholder engagement: Involving clinicians, administrators, and even potential end users in defining requirements ensures that solutions are not created in a vacuum.

Risk assessment tailored to healthcare: Prioritising risks such as patient data breaches, unforeseen clinical implications, or non-compliance with accessibility standards.

Prioritisation based on patient impact: DSDM's "MoSCoW" prioritisation (must have, should have, could have, won't have) has a unique meaning in healthcare. A "must have" is more than just attractive; it may affect patient safety.

Outline the iterative development plan: Foundations set the stage, but teams must recognise that the plan will grow inside the project's structure.

Let me provide you with a few examples:

Example 1: EHR Upgrade Project

Feasibility: Can vendor timelines coincide with IT staff availability? Are any present customisations incompatible and must be rebuilt? Is the budget feasible considering the scope of the project?

Foundations: Clinicians prioritise workflows, risking those that are most likely to cause interruption. Phased rollout plans prioritise units with the highest need or impact.

Example 2: Create a Telehealth Platform

FEASIBILITY

Can we provide adequate internet bandwidth and dependability in the desired service areas (particularly significant in rural contexts)?

How do we deal with the many state-level restrictions governing telemedicine prescribing and provider licensure?

Is there a patient population where telehealth could significantly improve access to care (underserved communities, individuals with limited mobility, etc.)?

FOUNDATIONS

Work with patients and professionals to identify key use cases (urgent care, chronic illness management, mental health).

The risk evaluation focuses on patient privacy, technological failure during a consultation, and ensuring that equitable access does not exacerbate the digital divide.

Outline a trial programme aimed at a certain population or service type, allowing for learning before full-scale deployment.

Example 3:   Public Health Campaign (Promote Flu Vaccination)

FEASIBILITY

Is the timeline consistent with flu season for optimum impact?

Is there data on which communities had low immunisation rates in the past, which could help prioritise efforts?

Are there reliable community partners (faith-based organisations, local clinics) who can help amplify messaging and alleviate hesitancy?

FOUNDATIONS

Co-design messaging with people of the target community to ensure that it is culturally appropriate and addresses specific needs.

Risk assessment considers the possibility of retaliation or the spread of misinformation. Prepare proactive responses.

Foundations establish a methodology for quickly measuring campaign effectiveness (by social media buzz and vaccination site data) in order to inform agile changes.

ADDITIONAL CONSIDERATIONS

Project size: Small projects may combine these phases, but the fundamental questions remain the same.

Urgency: A crisis response requires an expedited version. But even then, some feasibility is required: Is there any value in initiating a campaign if disinformation is already widespread?

Healthcare is complex. These examples are purposely simplified. A true EHR improvement project would include a long list of considerations for each phase.

KEY TAKEAWAYS

Healthcare cannot afford to skip these: The urge to rush to execution is tremendous. These phases ensure that you are heading in the right way from the outset.

Agile influence: Despite the DSDM framework, the ideas of collaboration and learning are incorporated in the project's early stages.

Defining Project Scope, Requirements, and Aligning to Healthcare Regulations

Thoroughness is essential in the early phases. It prevents scope creep, misaligned expectations, and other issues that could jeopardise patient safety or lead to non-compliance in the highly regulated healthcare industry.

Defining Project Scope

Broad but focused: Describe the project's broad goals and projected deliverables. In healthcare, link this to an organisation's strategic aim, such as increasing care results, efficiency, or patient experience.

What it is not: A thorough breakdown of each feature or task. DSDM's iterative approach allows specifics to emerge.

Such as: "Implement a new telehealth platform to expand access to primary care services within our existing patient population."

Gathering and Prioritising Requirements

Cross-functional collaboration is important in DSDM since it involves stakeholders. In healthcare, this means:

Clinicians define clinical requirements.

- IT outlines technical limits.
- Administrators emphasise feasibility and budgetary issues.
- Potential end users (if possible) offering insights regarding usability.

Prioritisation techniques: DSDM's MoSCoW (must, should, could, won't) paradigm is effective here:

■ Must have: Frequently linked to patient safety, fundamental functionality, or regulatory compliance.
■ Should have: Desirable, although the project can be completed without them initially.
■ Could have: Nice enhancements if time and finances allow.
■ Won't have: Explicitly out of scope for this project to avoid unreasonable expectations.

The Regulatory Factor

Identifying relevant regulations: Early involvement by compliance experts is critical. Examples are:
  – HIPAA for data privacy and FDA for medical devices/software.
  – State and local rules differ depending on the project.
"Baking in" compliance: Do not dismiss this as an afterthought. Regulatory needs become requirements (e.g., a medical device project may include a "must have" for audit logging).
Proactive risk management: One aspect of DSDM is being aware of what could derail the project. Missing a critical regulation jeopardises everything.

Tools and Techniques

User stories: Capture requirements in a patient-centred fashion. ("As a diabetic patient, I need to easily log my blood sugar readings in the app.")
Process mapping: Visually sketch workflows to evaluate how the solution fits, especially for projects that involve clinical practice.
Regulatory checklists: Create or use existing checklists that are tailored to your project type to ensure that nothing gets ignored.
Key point: This procedure is iterative, particularly in healthcare. New rules, evolving research, or preliminary testing may indicate the need to revise scope and standards.

Creating an Agile Project Roadmap and Release Plan

DSDM offers the overall framework for a healthcare project, while agile methodologies such as scrum and kanban drive implementation. A well-crafted roadmap and release plan promote alignment by focusing on value delivery throughout the project.

The High-Level Roadmap

Aligned with foundations: Draws on the project scope, high-level requirements, and major milestones established during the Foundations phase.
Timeboxing with a purpose: DSDM's timeboxes grow into larger portions on the roadmap. For example:
  – Three-month timeframe: Concentrate on establishing basic telehealth platform capabilities (secure video, chat, and appointment scheduling).
  – Later timebox: Add capabilities like e-prescribing and connectivity with patient records.
Visually communicative: The roadmap should be easy to understand for stakeholders with diverse degrees of technical expertise.

Detailed Release Planning

A release is a workable increment of the solution. Early releases may be internal or involve a small test group of people to gather immediate feedback.

Iteration driven: Within each roadmap timebox, scrum sprints or kanban workflows define smaller chunks of work and allow for adaptation.

Prioritisation is key: The release strategy should specify the "must have" features for each version. "Should haves" provide flexibility depending on learnings.

Healthcare caveat: Depending on the regulations, releases may not be as swift as with pure software. Consider testing and validation time.

Continuous Planning and Communication

The evolving roadmap: It is a framework, not a strict plan. Major modifications may still necessitate higher-level DSDM review, but it provides the flexibility required.

Release reviews: Each release is an opportunity to assess:
  – Did we provide value? (Not only did we meet the technical list.)
  – What does stakeholder feedback say about future priorities?
  – Are there any regulatory or other external factors that need to be addressed?

Transparency: Keep the roadmap visible. This demonstrates progress and underlines the project's iterative nature to stakeholders concerned about the lack of a large upfront plan.

Tools for Planning

Simple works: Spreadsheets and whiteboards can be useful, especially in the early phases.

Agile project management software, such as Jira and Trello, are ideal for precise sprint/task tracking and kanban visualisation.

Consider the healthcare context: Your tool must be flexible enough to support DSDM's review points as well as potentially higher documentation requirements for regulated projects.

Let me provide you with a hypothetical agile project roadmap and release plan

Project: *Creating a Patient Portal for Appointment Scheduling and Health Record Access*

High-level roadmap

Timebox 1 (3 months): Core portal functionality
  – Goals include secure patient login, rudimentary appointment booking, and the ability to examine laboratory results.
  – Alignment with foundations: Addresses the highest priority needs reported by doctors and patients.

Timebox 2 (3 months): Enhanced features
  – Goal: Enable medicine refill requests and secure messaging with providers.
  – Flexibility: The scope of secure messaging could be modified based on feedback/technical challenges in Timebox 1.

Timebox 3 (3 months): Increased integration and refinement
  – The goal is to integrate EHR (see more medical history) and provide patient education resources.
  – Heavily dependent on learnings: If regulatory barriers to EHR availability are significant, Timebox 3 may alter focus entirely.

Release plan (example of Timebox 1)

Release 1 (Sprints 1–2): Minimum viable portal
  – Must have: Secure login, basic profile editing, appointment viewing.
  – Should have: Limited appointment booking (just for primary care).
Release 2 (Sprints 3–4): Lab results
  – Must have: View test results and integrate with lab vendor system.
  – Should include: Plain English explanations of common test outcomes.
Release 3 (Sprints 5–6): Improved appointment booking
  – Must have: Features include the ability to book with numerous providers and examine appointment history.
  – Should have: Appointment reminders (SMS or email, depending on choice).

Additional notes

The first release might be to a select sample of tech-savvy patients to gather early feedback.

Regulation: A specific release may be dedicated to security testing or compliance certification.
Communication: The roadmap is shared with stakeholders, along with an explanation of the iterative release process, which aims for regular, useable increments.
Important: This is simplified. A real project would have more precise task breakdowns within sprints, as well as specified acceptance criteria for features. However, this demonstrates the balance between high-level direction (DSDM) and agile execution (sprint-driven releases).

Chapter 6

Iterative Development and Delivery

Adapting Scrum or Kanban Within DSDM's Framework

DSDM manages the overall project lifecycle, milestones, and high-level governance. Scrum and kanban provide complementary approaches for hands-on development execution during certain phases.

Scrum Within DSDM

Scrum sprints fit easily into the DSDM timeboxes. Each sprint works on a prioritised part of the broader deliverable during the timeframe established during foundations.

Roles: The DSDM roles (business sponsor, project manager, technical coordinator, etc.) correspond to scrum's product owner, scrum master, and development team, with some overlap.

Ceremonies include sprint planning, daily standups, reviews, and retrospectives, which promote focused development and continuous feedback on what works and what doesn't.

Where DSDM provides value: For larger projects, scrum alone may not provide sufficient strategic guidance. DSDM ensures that sprints are linked to the overarching healthcare-specific goal while keeping regulatory standards in mind.

Here are a few examples:

Example 1: Create a Patient Education App

DSDM foundation: Clearly defined scope (diabetes management), stakeholders identified (endocrinologists, app developers, etc.), and regulatory concerns addressed.

DSDM timebox: Three months for the original release. High-level functions are prioritised (blood sugar tracking, medication reminders, and diet content).

Scrum sprints:

Sprints 1–2: Core tracking features and safe login.

DOI: 10.4324/9781032688435-8

Sprints 3–4: Emphasis on medication reminders and interaction with pharmacy databases.
Sprints 5–6 create an initial collection of educational content and provide feedback mechanisms for patients to rate the information.
DSDM Review: At the end of the timebox, the working app is evaluated, as well as early input from a pilot group. This decides whether Timebox 2 expands content, includes more advanced tracking, and so on.

Example 2: Designing a Hospital Unit's Workflow

DSDM foundation: Target unit identified, pain points mapped, and desired objectives defined (e.g., reduce delays in patient discharge).
DSDM timebox: Two months dedicated to testing changes, collecting data, and assessing the impact.
Scrum sprints:
Sprints 1–2: Implemented a new room assignment method to speed up cleaning. Focused observation using pre/post change measures.
Sprints 3–4: Adjust the nurse call system to prioritise urgent requirements. Track response times and provide staff training.
DSDM review: Did Timebox 1's process adjustments have a meaningful impact on the main metric? Data informs the decision to refine, expand to additional units, or scrap failing concepts.

Example 3: Clinical Decision Support (CDS) Software

DSDM foundation: Targeted clinical area (drug-interaction alerts), technical requirements, and integration with EHR outlined.
Timeboxes for DSDM should correspond to validation steps.
Scrum sprints: For each validation step, prioritise core features. Regulatory paperwork requirements are converted into sprint tasks.
DSDM review: More formal than simply a demo. Has the CDS met accuracy standards? Were there usability issues that affected clinical workflow?

Kanban Within DSDM

Ideal for evolving requirements: Kanban's visualised workflow and emphasis on restricting work in progress (WIP) enable healthcare organisations to respond to unanticipated developments.
Bottleneck identification: The kanban board instantly indicates where work is stalled (waiting for regulatory expert input, clinical testing backlog).
Continuous delivery: While releases may not be as often as in other industries, kanban encourages delivering useful content as soon as they are completed, rather than waiting for a huge launch.
Where DSDM provides value: Kanban runs the risk of becoming bogged down in the details and losing sight of the big picture. DSDM's timeboxes and milestones keep the team focused on the overall project goals and deadlines.
Here are a few examples:

Example 1: Ongoing EHR Optimisation

DSDM foundation: A project that acknowledges that EHRs are not "set it and forget it." A dedicated staff is formed, and funds are provided for continual improvement and addressing user concerns.
Kanban board: Columns such as "requested," "in progress," "clinician testing," "ready for rollout," and "completed."

Evolving requirements: New issues are regularly added as cards (frustrating order entry process, require a new report type). Prioritisation is flexible.

Bottleneck identification: A pile-up in "clinician testing" indicates that not enough staff time is given to feedback, necessitating a solution either within the team or at the DSDM level.

Continuous delivery: Small tweaks, new order sets, and other changes are delivered live as they become available, eliminating the need for large disruptive updates.

Example 2: Public Health Outreach Campaign

DSDM foundation: The campaign's broad goal (to increase immunisation) is established, and a high-level timeline exists; but, messaging and strategies may need to alter quickly.

Kanban board: Columns such as "content ideas," "in development," "A/B testing," "launched," and "metrics review." WIP limits require prioritisation.

Evolving requirements: News of vaccination negative effects emerges. The board immediately identifies what is presently available and needs to be revised, as well as where new content efforts should be focused.

Bottleneck identification: A high number of cards stuck in "metrics review" suggests that either the team lacks data analytics expertise or incorrect data are being collected.

Continuous delivery: Social media postings, flyers, and other marketing materials are launched as soon as they pass testing. This enables the response to real-time public mood.

Example 3: Medical Device Development (Software Component)

DSDM foundation: The device has a stated scope, although feature prioritisation may change depending on early user input or regulatory changes.

Kanban board: Tracks feature development but also includes columns such as "regulatory review," "usability testing Round 1," and "bug fixes."

Evolving requirements: FDA feedback requires a redesign. WIP limitations ensure that the core device continues to progress while accommodating new work.

Bottleneck identification: If too many features stall in the "regulatory review" stage, it indicates that legal/compliance participation is required sooner.

Continuous delivery: The software's limited internal rollouts enable speedy fixes. Kanban here prevents a "big bang" launch that could overload users.

Choosing Scrum Versus Kanban (or a Hybrid)

Project type: Scrum is a suitable fit if the requirements are well-defined upfront and the team can commit to deliverables within a timeframe.

Unpredictability: If you are dealing with a large number of prospective regulatory changes or need flexibility around jobs that depend on clinician availability, kanban's adaptability may be preferable.

Team experience: Scrum's established framework makes it an easier starting point for teams new to agile. Experienced teams could benefit from kanban's flexibility.

Let's use healthcare-specific examples to highlight the decision-making process between scrum and kanban:

Scenario 1: A Mobile App for Symptom Tracking

Well-defined scope: Patients with a specified chronic disease will track symptoms, receive reminders, and securely communicate information with their doctor.

Predictable workflow: While app development involves unknowns, the basic elements are obvious and unlikely to alter significantly owing to laws.

Team mix: While developers are used to agile, this is the first time clinicians have been actively involved in a project team.

Scrum is probably the best fit. Sprints provide concentration, defined roles assist the team in finding its rhythm, and the app's scope is manageable enough for timebox planning.

Scenario 2: Addressing an Emerging Infectious Disease

Unpredictable requirements: Scientific guidance advances frequently, public health messages must alter quickly, and resources may be shifted abruptly.

A task could be data analysis one day and build a vaccine drive-thru the next. Clinician availability is contingent on the ever-changing situation.

Team under pressure: Everyone is probably out of their comfort zone. Adding the rigour of scrum to the natural tension is likely to backfire.

Choice: Kanban is preferable. The emphasis turns to regulating the flow of the most critical tasks, identifying bottlenecks, and avoiding burnout.

Scenario 3: Large-Scale EHR Implementation

The overall plan is complex but phased (it will be implemented module by module). Each module's requirements are well-defined.

Dependency on others: The vendor, hospital IT, and other factors all contribute significantly to success. Delays may occur due to factors outside the project team's control.

Team experience: A combination of agile-savvy developers and waterfall-experienced implementation professionals.

Hybrid is a viable option. DSDM structure at the highest level, scrum for modules with a defined scope, and a kanban-style workflow to manage issues and dependencies that could derail sprints.

Important: These are only beginning points, not strict restrictions. The challenge of the app project in Scenario 1 may appeal to a team with extensive kanban experience. Realistically, it is about determining the strategy that will best assist the team in attaining the specific goals of their healthcare endeavour.

Prioritising User Stories with a Focus on Patient and Clinician Needs

In healthcare projects, user stories extend beyond technical functionality. They serve as a link between the solution being developed and how it actually enhances the care experience for both clinicians and patients.

Understanding the "Why" of User Stories

Patient focused: A user story is more than merely "As a patient, I want to view my lab results." It solves the following issues: "As a patient with chronic anxiety, I want to view my lab results before my appointment so I can prepare questions for my doctor."

Focus of the clinician: "As a nurse, I want to see a patient's recent medication changes quickly so I can provide safe care." Consider the following:

 - Reducing the time spent searching for information.
 - Increasing their ability to make educated care decisions.
 - Reducing the risk of errors caused by fragmented data

Prioritisation Techniques With a Healthcare Lens

MoSCoW revisited: This DSDM standard develops traction in healthcare:
- Must have: It has a direct influence on patient safety (drug allergy alerts), may result in significant inefficiencies, or meets a vital regulatory requirement.
- Patients' quality of life should be significantly improved, as should professionals' workflows.
- Could have been nice enhancements if resources allowed.
- Will not have: Explicitly out of scope to avoid unreasonable expectations.

Involve users in prioritisation. Workshops in which patients or clinicians help rank prospective user stories based on their real-world impact are effective.

Can development team members "walk a mile" in the user's shoes? Observing a doctor struggle with the present system, as well as conducting patient interviews (when ethically appropriate), can help establish this insight.

Prioritisation as Dialogue

Avoid the "wish list" trap: Early user stories may be broad. The conversation refines them: "You want easier appointment booking ... is the problem with finding open slots, the process being confusing, or something else entirely?"

Technical feasibility matters: A patient may seek a functionality that is simply not possible with existing technologies. This should be stated gently, with alternate approaches to addressing the root pain point considered.

Prioritisation is ongoing. Feedback on a deployed increment may reveal that an apparently minor user story has a significant impact ... or that a highly anticipated one fails to meet expectations.

Let me provide you with a few examples:

Example 1: EHR Medication Module

A must have user story: "As a physician, I want to see a clear, visually distinct alert if a medication I'm prescribing has a dangerous interaction with the patient's existing medications."

A could have user story: "As a patient, I want to see potential medication side effects translated into plain language."

Balancing the two: The alarm cannot be negotiated. However, if resources are limited, substantial side effect information may need to be released later, particularly if complicated data sourcing is required.

Example 2: Patient Portal

Must haves: "As a patient with limited mobility, I want the option to schedule a telehealth appointment with my provider so I can get care without needing to travel." (It addresses accessibility and the possibility for better outcomes.)

Should include the following user story: "As a patient, I want to receive appointment reminders via my preferred method (text, email, phone call) to reduce the chance of missing appointments." (It improves care continuity; nonetheless, workarounds exist.)

Could include a user story: "As a patient, I want to be able to upload photos of a skin rash or other concern for my doctor to review ahead of the appointment." (Potential for convenience, but privacy and technological issues may arise.)

Example 3: The CDS Tool for Early Sepsis Detection

Must Have: "As an ER nurse, I want a clear alert that highlights a patient's increasing risk of sepsis based on real-time vital sign trends and lab results." (This aligns with the key patient safety priority.)

Should include a user narrative: "As a physician, I want the CDS alert to provide links to evidence-based treatment guidelines relevant to the patient's specific conditions." (This supports decision-making but does not need quick action.)

May have a user story: "As a hospital administrator, I want the CDS to track metrics on how often alerts are acted upon, to assess the tool's impact." (Useful for ROI analysis, but not fundamental functionality.)

Example 4: Designing a Hospital Waiting Area

Must have: "As a patient with sensory sensitivities, I want a designated quiet space in the waiting area where I can avoid overwhelming noise and lighting." (Addressing accessibility needs.)

Should include the following user story: "As a parent with young children, I want a safe and contained play area within sight of the waiting area seating." (This improves patient experience substantially.)

Could have. "As a patient, I want access to real-time updates on estimated wait times for my appointment." (A nice advantage, but the cost of technology may outweigh the benefits.)

Key takeaways

Healthcare settings are diverse: The "must-haves" vary dramatically depending on whether it's a high-acuity ER project or a patient wellness app.

Think beyond the initial user: Even though the user narrative is told from the perspective of a nurse, the sepsis CDS has an influence on nurses, doctors, and, ultimately, patients.

"Won't have" matters: If a waiting room makeover cannot include private rooms for infectious patients, mention this clearly to minimise disappointment later.

Managing Changes and Continuous Improvement in the Healthcare Environment

Healthcare projects rarely have the luxury of a completely predictable route. Agile approaches, which are inherent in the DSDM framework, offer ways to view change as an opportunity for refinement rather than an impediment to overcome.

Adopting an Iterative Mindset

Small, frequent adjustments: Iterative development, which is central to both DSDM and agile, reduces the impact of change. It's the difference between course correcting a tiny boat and a large ship.

Feedback loops: Each sprint, release, or DSDM review point yields fresh data. This could be a good thing ("This feature is more popular than we thought!") or a bad thing ("The regulation update means we need to rethink this entire module").

Change as learning: Agile's emphasis on retrospectives entails examining not only what was delivered, but also how the team responded to changing needs. This promotes resilience in future initiatives.

Proactive Change Management

DSDM's role: Agile is adaptive, but DSDM provides oversight. Major changes in scope or timeframe still require appropriate levels of assessment and approval.

Transparent communication: Changes should not be a surprise. Stakeholders must grasp the "why" behind a pivot and how it fits into the overall project goals.

The ripple effect: In healthcare, even minor changes can have a significant influence on many systems or operations. This must be evaluated promptly.

Continuous Improvement Is a Core Value

Beyond the project: The DSDM "deployment" phase, combined with agile's emphasis on continuous learning, ensures that the mentality is not "done" and then forgotten.

Data as a driver: Did the new workflow genuinely increase efficiency? Do patients use the gateway as intended? Collecting post-release metrics is critical.

Culture of improvement: Teams should feel free to suggest changes even outside of formal retrospectives. This prevents the "good enough" mentality.

Healthcare-Specific Considerations

Regulatory shifts: Projects require a strategy for assessing and integrating regulatory changes. This may demand specific duties or a "regulatory buffer" in timetables.

User adoption: Even the best technical solution will fail if physicians and patients do not use it. Change management is a component of continuous improvement that helps to increase adoption and address issues.

Balancing innovation and safety healthcare cannot be completely risk-averse. Agile methodologies enable you to test new ideas in a controlled environment and discover the perfect balance.

Let me illustrate with a few examples:

Example 1: Public Health Texting Campaign

Initial plan: Messages will focus on vaccine facts. DSDM review points enable metric analysis (e.g., click-through rates).

The change: Data suggest that engagement is poor, yet SMS asking consumers if they have any questions receive responses. Campaigns pivot to answer concerns rather than simply broadcasting information.

Continuous improvement: Even after the campaign, the team analyses what worked. Were certain themes more successful? This helps to inform future health efforts.

Example 2: Create a Symptom Tracking App for Cancer Patients

Initial plan: The primary focus is on core tracking (pain, nausea, etc.), encrypted chat with their oncology team, and basic instructional content.

The change: Early user response indicates that patients really seek a means to connect with one another. A monitored community component should be considered.

Continuous improvement: User compliance with the app varies. Was the onboarding process too complex? Do the reminder notifications need to be adjusted? These granular data are equally important as feature development.

Example 3: Hospital-Wide Rollout of a New EHR System

Initial plan: Phased rollout by unit, comprehensive staff training, and deployment of go-live support teams were the initial plan.

The change: A vital workflow for a given specialisation just does not function in the new system. This could cause a delay in the overall rollout unless a solution or workaround is developed promptly.

Continuous improvement: Even after installation, complications will arise. A feedback platform that allows employees to readily submit complaints (rather than merely helpdesk requests) is required, transforming dissatisfaction into actionable improvements.

Example 4: Designing a Clinic Waiting Area

The initial plan focuses on new furniture, relaxing paint colours, and a designated children's play area.

The change: According to our observations, many patients are using their phones while waiting. Adding charging stations may be a little expense with a significant impact on satisfaction.

Continuous improvement: Patient surveys after redesign should not simply inquire if they like it. Do wait times seem shorter? Is it easier for people with disabilities to navigate? These data inform future modifications.

Key takeaways

Scope of change: Examples range from a significant shift in campaign approach to the relatively small installation of charging stations. Agile methodologies can scale to both.

Healthcare is human: Sometimes technical changes are required, while other times emotional needs are addressed (patients feel heard; professionals are not overwhelmed).

Metrics matter, but so does observation: Data are important, but so is the ability to just witness the solution in action. Agile's emphasis on working solutions allows you to identify gaps that spreadsheets may miss.

Chapter 7

Collaboration and Communication for Success

Effective Communication Strategies With Patients, Clinicians, and Stakeholders

Let's look at how to design communication methods for success in healthcare projects, so that patients, clinicians, and a wide range of stakeholders feel informed, involved, and understood.

Effective Communication Strategies for Patients, Clinicians, and Stakeholders

DSDM recognises that open collaboration and communication are essential for obtaining excellent outcomes in complicated healthcare undertakings. Here's how to make this happen:

Communicate With Patients

Empathy and accessibility: Avoid using jargon and technical words. Consider how the initiative will significantly improve their care experience. Consider health literacy levels while developing products.

Respect for privacy: Provide explicit information about how patient data will be gathered, used, and protected. Maintain transparency about the measures in place.

Two-way channels: Don't merely broadcast information to patients. Create feedback tools (surveys, focus groups, as needed) to ensure their perspectives are heard within the project's restrictions.

Diversity and inclusion: Is written information translated for your patients? Are visual aids usable by people with disabilities? Inclusivity is vital in healthcare communication.

DOI: 10.4324/9781032688435-9

Communicating With Clinicians

Value their time: Updates should be brief and focused on the impact on their workflow. Avoid meetings that may have been completed via email or a fast update on a collaborative platform.

Emphasise "why": Clinicians are more inclined to embrace change if they understand how the project contributes to better patient care, rather than just another technical task to fulfil.

Listen actively: Their thoughts from the ground are invaluable. Feedback should feel like a conversation, not a directive.

Manage expectations: Be clear about what won't change and the project's constraints. This avoids disappointment and increases trust.

Communicate With Stakeholders

Tailor your message: A project sponsor is interested in high-level progress towards milestones. An IT team member requires detailed reports on anticipated technical issues. A regulator wants to see proof of compliance.

Visual communication: DSDM's roadmaps, process diagrams, and other tools are extremely effective. Make them visually clear and understandable to non-technical audiences.

Proactive risk reporting: Stakeholders should not be surprised by difficulties. Present viable mitigation techniques alongside the open framing of hazards.

Celebrate successes: Recognising team successes and their beneficial influence on patient care increases morale and reinforces the importance of collaboration.

Healthcare-specific considerations

Patient confidentiality: Any communication using case examples must strictly preserve privacy (even if anonymised, specifics can be identified).

Clinicians' schedules: Asynchronous communication tools may be necessary. A brief, well-organised video update that they may watch on their own time may be preferable to attempting to bring them live for a meeting.

Regulatory language: If you're working with an agency like the FDA, learn about their preferred communication techniques and the forms of documents they want.

Tools and techniques

- Meeting agendas and minutes should remain focused, even during informal stand-ups.
- Shared collaboration platforms enable asynchronous updates, eliminating meeting overload.
- Consider using infographics, short movies, and other patient-facing materials in addition to text.
- Progress dashboards are visual and easily available to relevant stakeholders.

Let's look at communication problems in a project that involves direct patient contact and ethical patient feedback methods.

Project Example: Public Health Initiative Promoting Home Blood Pressure Monitoring

The goal is to enhance hypertension management, particularly in underprivileged communities. This includes distributing blood pressure cuffs, conducting an educational campaign, and maybe developing an app for patients to log readings.

Communication challenges

- Health literacy and trust: Messaging must be simple, jargon-free, and address any scepticism of the healthcare system. Simply instructing people to monitor is insufficient; it must also explain why it is important in an understandable manner.
- Digital divide: An app-focused solution excludes a portion of the intended audience. Communication must include several channels (phone, paper logs, etc.), and the project itself must address the equity issue, possibly through collaboration with community centres.
- Disinformation: This topic is probably riddled with disinformation on social media. The campaign must proactively fight this by collaborating with reputable community voices.
- Reaching the right people: Where does your target population obtain health information? Putting flyers up only in doctors' offices will not suffice. Community ties are essential for successful outreach.

Techniques for ethical patient feedback

- Focus groups: These can be effective in the early phases of understanding concerns and tailoring messages. Compensation for participants' time is vital, as is ensuring that the group is demographically diverse.
- Short, easily accessible surveys embedded in the app (if applicable), delivered in collaboration with community groups, etc. Make these multilingual and provide opportunities for participation even if you don't have access to technology.
- Community advisory board: A small sample of patients representing the target community can provide continual feedback, ensuring that the initiative remains focused on their actual requirements.
- Privacy emphasis: Be extremely upfront about how data are used. Do not make "sharing with clinicians" the default; instead, require patients to opt in.

Ethical considerations

- Institutional Review Board (IRB) approval: If the input is considered research, this may be required. Consider this when planning your timelines.
- Vulnerable populations: Extra precautions are required when working with minors, people with cognitive disabilities, and so on.
- Not just gathering feedback, but acting on it: Patients will get disillusioned if their input does not result in tangible changes to the project.

Additional notes

- The power of storytelling: Sharing anonymous success stories about how the programme helped someone can be more powerful than simply providing data.
- Feedback on feedback: Did the surveys seem too long? Was the focus group location difficult to travel to? This meta-feedback makes the project more inclusive.

Let's take on the difficulty of communicating with physicians in a way that encourages buy-in, even if the project has the potential to increase their burden.

Scenario: A hospital-wide initiative to improve sepsis detection and early intervention.

This is expected to include adjustments to clinician workflow, the implementation of a new clinical decision support tool, and changed documentation requirements.

Why clinician buy-in is hard (and essential)

- Burnout is real: Simply asking people to do more creates resistance. Projects must admit that this exists.

- They've seen it before: Fancy tools that don't deliver in the real world leave them sceptical. They have to believe this is different.
- They prioritise the impact on patient care. You must draw the dots between the project workload and its good impact on the patients to whom it is committed.

Communication strategies

- Early involvement: Do not offer them with a completed strategy. Have clinicians help outline the pain issues that the project aims to solve. This encourages ownership.
- Focus on the problem, not just the solution. Don't start with, "We're launching this new tool." Start by saying "Missed sepsis cases are increasing, let's work together to figure out why."
- Workflow, workflow, workflow! Avoid abstract benefits. Show them how the project will save them time (e.g., by automating elements of the present documentation process) or prevent them from being woken up at night by false alarms.
- Champions and sceptics: Identify influential clinicians who are likely to support the project and allow them to speak with their colleagues. Engage with people known to be resistant; their concerns are likely echoed by many.
- Phased rollout and feedback: Allow for physician feedback to help modify processes before system-wide introduction. This fosters trust and makes the transition less stressful.

Communication isn't magic

Even the best communication cannot save a fundamentally bad project. Consider:

- Dedicated project resources: Can some of the existing clinical documentation burden be temporarily decreased to allow for project work?
- Training that fits their reality: Short, on-demand modules that they can access throughout a shift are preferable to lengthy mandated classes.
- Celebrating the wins: Highlight situations where the new workflow detected early sepsis that a human could have missed. This reinforces the reason for the endeavour.

Collaborative Decision-Making Techniques

Let's look at how DSDM and agile techniques promote a collaborative decision-making environment, which is essential for navigating the intricacies of healthcare projects.

Collaborative Decision-Making Techniques

While DSDM provides a project framework, agile methodologies that empower teams and stakeholders improve decision-making within that structure.

1. Facilitated workshops
   - Purpose: This is ideal for the early stages of a project (issue description, solution exploration) or when a significant course adjustment is required.
   - The facilitator's role: They guarantee that different views are heard, that no single member dominates, and that the group moves towards actionable outcomes.
   - Techniques: Brainstorming, prioritisation matrices, and affinity mapping (grouping related ideas) help maintain the process orderly even when debates become heated.

- Healthcare example: A session with clinicians, IT, and patient reps to determine the "must-haves" for a new patient portal reveals dramatically diverse priorities.
2. Transparency and information sharing
   - The foundation of collaboration: Decisions made in secret engender suspicion. The project team should have access to relevant data, such as meeting minutes.
   - Tools include collaborative whiteboards (Miro, for example), wikis, and even a simple shared document that can serve as a knowledge repository.
   - Balancing with the need to know: Patient privacy, sensitive regulatory information, and so on may need to be restricted. Understand what may and cannot be shared.
3. Consensus-driven versus DSDM decision points
   - The nuance: Agile teams frequently strive for consensus. DSDM recognises that certain individuals (such as the business sponsor) must make decisions on occasion.
   - Hybrid is possible: A team may achieve an agreement on lower-level choices, with the understanding that larger differences will be escalated to the appropriate DSDM review point.
   - Why consensus matters: When a decision is owned by the group, implementation goes more smoothly. Dictates from high places provoke resistance.
4. Embrace the retrospective
   - Beyond task completion: Agile retrospectives focus on how the team collaborated, not just what was delivered. This includes investigating how decisions were reached.
   - Spotting patterns: Was the team paralysed by its attempt to reach complete consensus? Did a leader's rapid, imperfect decision have favourable results?
   - Iterating on the process: The team might suggest changes to their decision-making for the following sprint or project phase.

Healthcare Considerations

- Clinician schedules: Asynchronous decision-making tools may be required (voting on alternatives, commenting on proposed solutions).
- External input: Decisions affecting regulations may necessitate a formal review process with a regulatory agency outside the main project team.
- Do not confuse collaboration with lack of accountability: DSDM still has defined responsibilities. The idea is to make better decisions based on input rather than avoiding accountability.

Let's look at workshop facilitation approaches as well as tactics for dealing with difficult situations where consensus appears to be out of reach.

Facilitation Techniques for Workshops

1. **Dot voting** is most effective for prioritising choices, such as patient portal features or workflow redesign pain points.
   - How it works: Each participant receives a specified amount of "dot" stickers. They place these on the alternatives that they believe are most essential. This instantly visualises areas of strong agreement and identifies outliers.
   - Healthcare twist: Perform numerous rounds with various coloured dots indicating different roles. Does IT prioritise ease of integration, whilst physicians connect the dots depending on possible impact on patient care? This indicates surface misalignment.

2. **Round-robin brainstorming** is ideal for generating new ideas early in a project or when stalled.
   - How it works: One person starts, and everyone shares an idea in turn. There will be no judgement or discussion at this time. Initially, the goal is quantity rather than quality.
   - Facilitator's role: Keep things going. If someone is apprehensive, gently prompt them with an open-ended question related to the issue. Write everything, including seemingly absurd thoughts.
3. **Impact versus effort matrix**
   - Best for: Moving beyond "wouldn't it be nice" features and focusing on what is doable within the project scope.
   - How it works: A big grid with one axis labelled "impact" and the other labelled "effort". Ideas are placed (sticky notes are great). This drives difficult decisions: Is something with huge impact but massive work worthwhile?
   - Healthcare twist: Create a third axis for "risk". This could include risks to patient safety, regulatory compliance, and so on.

Managing conflicting priorities.

1. Back to the "why" stakeholders may disagree on solutions, but focusing on the primary problem the initiative seeks to address can discover common ground.
2. Data as a neutral arbiter: "I think patients will hate that" is less persuasive than even a small-scale usability test demonstrating that a feature is perplexing.
3. The pilot/experiment: Can two competing solutions be tried on a small scale? This converts opinions into usable data for future decisions.
4. Transparent escalation: The DSDM structure is useful here. Higher-level review points are used when a team is unable to resolve an impasse. However, they should present the options examined rather than simply dumping the problem upstairs.

Important note: Even the best tactics will fail if the workshop is badly planned. Consider:

- The right people: Too many attendees hinder discussion. Too few, and you lack the necessary viewpoints.
- Prep work: An agenda and pre-reading save time on basic information that could be delivered asynchronously.
- Follow-up: Workshop results aren't magic. Someone needs to turn those sticky notes into action items within a specific deadline.

The best workshop technique depends on the precise outcome you want. Here's a summary of some typical aims and approaches suitable for achieving them (Table 7.1).

Remember:

- Combine techniques: Don't be scared to employ several techniques throughout a workshop. Begin with brainstorming, then move on to dot voting on the best ideas, etc.
- Consider the group size. Some strategies, such as affinity mapping, are more effective with smaller groups that allow for in-depth discussion.
- Adapt to the project stage. Early brainstorming workshops may require very different activities than a later-stage workshop aimed at finalising user stories.

Table 7.1   Workshop Goals and Techniques

Workshop Goal	Technique	Why it Works
Generate a large number of creative ideas	Round-robin brainstorming	Encourages participation and prevents early judgment, fostering a flow of unique ideas.
Identify key areas for improvement	Affinity mapping	Groups similar ideas together, revealing underlying themes and common pain points.
Prioritise a list of features or solutions	Dot voting	Facilitates quick decision-making and highlights areas of agreement amongst the group.
Evaluate solutions based on feasibility	Impact versus effort matrix	Provides a visual framework for balancing potential impact with the resources needed to implement it.
Develop a shared understanding of a problem	Case study analysis	Discussing a real-world scenario sparks conversation and allows participants to connect with the project's purpose.
Refine existing processes	User journey mapping	Visually depicts a user's experience, helping pinpoint areas for improvement in a healthcare context (e.g., patient flow through an emergency department).

Troubleshooting: Common Workshop Challenges the Dominating Participant

A participant assuming control of the discussion can derail a workshop. Here are some options for addressing this:

- Establish ground rules upfront: At the start of the session, briefly state the expectations, such as respecting others' time and encouraging everyone to take part.
- Direct questions for others: When the dominating participant speaks, use phrases like "That's a great point, what do others think?" or "I'd love to hear from someone who hasn't spoken yet."
- Use techniques that promote equality: Techniques such as round-robin brainstorming or silent writing, in which everyone writes down their thoughts before sharing them, might help level the field.
- Private conversations: If the behaviour continues, you can have a courteous, private talk with the individual after the session to emphasise its influence on group dynamics.

Additional tips:

- Begin with an icebreaker: A short exercise at the start can make attendees feel more comfortable speaking out.
- Maintain eye contact with quieter individuals and respond to nonverbal cues (raised brows, etc.).
- Be flexible: If a technique does not work, be willing to adjust and try something new.

You can transform workshops into productive sessions that capitalise on your team's collective intelligence by employing the proper approaches and solving frequent difficulties!

Leveraging Technology for Communication and Knowledge Sharing

Let's look at how to strategically employ technology to improve communication and knowledge exchange in healthcare projects.

Utilising technology for communication and knowledge sharing.

In the complicated and sometimes geographically scattered world of healthcare, technology is critical to facilitating effective collaboration. Here's how to use it effectively:

1. Collaboration platforms
   - Central hubs: Select systems (such as Slack, Microsoft Teams, or healthcare-specific solutions) that enable real-time and asynchronous collaboration.
   - Structured channels: To keep discussions focused, organise communication around certain subjects (e.g., "EHR integration," "patient feedback," and "regulatory updates").
   - Keep accessibility in mind: Make sure the platform is easy to use and compatible with many devices.
2. Project and knowledge management tools
   - Beyond email and spreadsheets, tools like Jira, Trello, and Confluence may help you monitor tasks, visualise timelines, and create a living archive of project choices.
   - The power of search: A cluttered SharePoint folder is worthless. A well-organised wiki allows someone to rapidly access the information they need, even if they were not involved in the original work.
   - Workflow integration: If possible, have these tools connect to your communication platform, decreasing the need to switch between platforms.
3. Document sharing and co-editing
   - Real-time collaboration: Cloud-based document solutions (such as Google Docs) help to develop consensus and avoid version control issues.
   - Comment and revision history: Track how a choice evolved, making it easy for someone new to the project to get up to speed.
   - Security and compliance: Ensure that your chosen solution complies with any healthcare-specific standards governing sensitive data.
4. Virtual meetings and workshops
   - When presence matters: Video conferencing (Zoom, Webex, etc.) is critical for developing relationships, particularly with remote team members.
   - Interactive features: Use screen sharing, virtual whiteboards, and polls to increase involvement and duplicate in-person workshop activities as closely as possible.
   - Don't over-rely: Brief asynchronous updates in a collaborative platform can frequently eliminate the need for another meeting.

Healthcare-specific considerations

- Telehealth integration: Can the same platform be utilised for quick check-ins with patients or external partners, reducing context switching?

■ Data security: Prioritise Health Insurance Portability and Accountability Act (HIPAA)-compliant solutions and ensure the team is properly trained to protect sensitive information.

■ Clinician workflow: Avoid solutions that require several clicks within the EHR or frequent logins to separate systems.

Beyond technology: Fostering a culture of sharing

■ Lead by example: If project managers solely communicate using formal documentation, the team will follow suit. Use the cooperation platform actively.

■ Celebrate knowledge sharing: Recognise team members who provide useful resources or are prepared to answer others' inquiries.

■ Make it routine: Add "sharing updates" to sprint reviews or team meetings.

Strategies to Encourage the Adoption of Collaboration Tools in Healthcare

Transitioning from traditional, although obsolete, communication methods to new collaborative platforms necessitates a deliberate approach, particularly in a varied healthcare organisation. Here are some ideas to win over folks who are used to "old-school" methods:

1. Address concerns front on.
   - Understand their pain points: What are clinicians concerned about losing when using the new tools? Is it convenience, fear of information overload, or scepticism that "yet another login" can enhance workflow?
   - Targeted communication: Do not send out generic emails. Customise communications to suit the unique issues of each user group (physicians, nurses, and administrative personnel).
2. Focus on benefits, not just features.
   - Show, don't tell: Physicians inundated with emails may dismiss "improved communication." Show how the platform may improve secure messaging with coworkers or even patients.
   - Quantify the value proposition: Can these tools reduce the time spent looking for information or missing messages from specialists? Use real-world examples to demonstrate the time-saving benefits.
3. User-centred training and support
   - Keep it short and actionable: Busy healthcare workers do not require hour-long webinars. Focus on bite-sized training modules that highlight the main functionalities most important to their role.
   - Superuser network: Identify early adopters who can promote the platform among their divisions, answer queries, and resolve small concerns.
   - Readily available support: A specialised IT support person or easily accessible FAQs can help folks who are new to technology.
4. Begin small, scale up
   - Pilot programme: Start with a tiny, less critical project or department. Success stories and great feedback from early adopters can be extremely motivating.
   - Phased rollout: As users become more comfortable and accustomed to the platform, more features will be introduced gradually. Avoid overwhelming users with too much information at once.

5. Lead by example.
- Executive buy-in is critical: Leadership's public endorsement of the new tools underlines the necessity of employing them.
- Walk the walk: If leadership continues to rely primarily on email or paper communication, clinicians are unlikely to embrace modern tools.

Managing Privacy Concerns in an Open Communication Culture

■ Transparency and education: Explain how the platform secures patient data. Ensure that all users understand the HIPAA compliance rules and their role in information security.

■ Role-based access control: Control access to sensitive data based on job function. Not everyone has to see everything.

■ Audit trail and logging: Keep detailed logs of who accessed what information, when, and why. This prevents misuse and offers a safety net.

■ Open communication channels: Create an environment in which employees feel empowered to report concerns about potential privacy violations without fear of retaliation.

Finding the Right Balance

Open communication is essential for teamwork, but so is patient confidentiality. By prioritising these tactics, you may establish a digital workspace that promotes knowledge sharing while protecting sensitive health information.

Additional Notes

■ Consider providing incentives (such as continuing education credits) to encourage early adoption.

■ Make the platform entertaining and engaging! Healthcare can be serious, but collaboration tools do not need to be. To add a personal touch, look at options like emoticons and custom avatar creation.

Let's look at ways to personalise collaboration solutions to unique healthcare cooperation demands while also overcoming communication barriers in large organisations.

Designing Collaboration Tools for Specific Teams

Geographically dispersed specialists:

■ Emphasis on asynchronous: Differences in time zones make real-time meetings impossible. Tools with robust commenting/threaded conversations enable input even when everyone is not online at the same time.

■ Virtual consultations: Can the technology support secure video chats for brief patient-case discussions? This encourages collaboration without having to plan schedules for a full-fledged meeting.

■ Integration is key: Can experts simply use the platform alongside their EHR? When people's time is valuable, reducing clicks is important.

Interdisciplinary care teams (hospital settings):

■ Role-specific alerts: While everyone requires a general project channel, customisable notifications reduce overload. A nurse does not need to review every new budget sheet, but she should be notified of changed care plans immediately.

■ Secure messaging with context: Replacing pagers with in-platform chat allows you to ask brief inquiries about a specific patient and their history, rather than just "call me."

■ Patient involvement (when appropriate): If the platform allows, can patients (or their carers) have limited access to check test results or convey non-urgent questions to their team?

Public health research collaboration:

■ Data sharing focus: The tool should be able to handle massive datasets with ease, maybe including visualisation features.

■ External partner access: Consider platforms intended for research collaboration that can accept those outside the core organisation while maintaining appropriate security controls.

■ Version control is life: Tracking changes to documents and databases over time is critical as research findings emerge.

Unique Challenges in Large Healthcare Organisations

■ Siloed departments: A tool will not magically enable collaboration. Leadership must incentivise its use for cross-departmental communication, not simply among established teams.

■ Legacy systems: New tools must "play nice" with frequently obsolete EHRs and other basic systems. Early IT engagement is critical for avoiding technological bottlenecks.

■ Regulatory complexity: A small clinic faces fewer challenges. Large organisations must ensure that the tool and how it is utilised comply with a variety of rules, which may change over time.

■ Training at scale: It can't be merely one-time webinars. Make resources available on demand and searchable, and recognise the importance of continuing onboarding when personnel turnover happens.

Breaking down divisions across major healthcare organisations is a difficult but critical goal, and collaboration platforms can play an important role. Here are some techniques for encouraging their use and creating a coherent culture:

1. Connect the platform to meaningful outcomes

– Avoid the phrase "we got the cool tool, now use it" and instead concentrate on particular interdepartmental pain problems that the platform can address. Did a delay in lab results reaching the appropriate physician result in negative outcomes? Show how the platform can prevent this.

– Target early wins: Identify small-scale projects where traditional communication methods are plainly failing, and the platform's benefits will be readily apparent. Success creates enthusiasm.

– Tie to organisational goals: If the organisation is focused on improving the "patient experience," demonstrate how the tools can help with better handoffs, minimising patients' feelings of being bounced about.

2. Encourage the right behaviours

- Gamification does not have to be cheesy. Simple leaderboards that recognise teams with the most collaboration tool engagement, or badges for those who routinely answer promptly, can foster a sense of friendly competition.
- Time Back: Determine how much time is saved by using the platform to overcome irritating communication barriers. Leadership acknowledging this saved time is important for a staff that is continually pushed.
- Mentorship and recognition: Connect tech-savvy employees with those who are struggling to adopt. Turn knowledge sharing into a skill that is valued alongside clinical performance.

3. The power of storytelling

- "A picture is worth…" Create before/after process maps to visualise the impact. Display the complicated path a pharmaceutical order presently takes versus the streamlined approach in the new tool.
- Patient stories: When relevant, describe how improved collaboration (facilitated by the tool) resulted in better care – "Because the specialist saw the lab result right away, they were able to…" Remember that healthcare providers are driven by their patients.
- Celebrate collaboration wins: Did the platform's easy cross-departmental collaboration help resolve a complex situation quickly? Highlight this in newsletters, etc., emphasising that the tool was the facilitator.

4. Executive sponsorship: Make or break it

- Mandates backfire: Instead, have high-level executives publicly use the tool and refer to it in meetings. "I saw your comment on the project plan, let's discuss…" is a strong statement.
- Make it a leadership key performance indicator (KPI). If a department head's performance review includes how successfully they've helped their staff adopt and use the platform, it sends a strong message.
- Address concerns: Senior employees may be concerned that the tool will expose their lack of technological expertise. It is critical to provide targeted support while emphasising that the goal is better outcomes rather than who can type the fastest.

Important notes:

- Don't underestimate inertia: Some people will always oppose change. Concentrate on winning over the "movable middle," and when their success becomes apparent, the resistors will be ostracised.
- Feedback loop: Does the tool actually work? Gather honest feedback to see where it is effective and where it requires improvement before people become disillusioned.

Let's look at a basic silo-induced dilemma and how a collaborative platform can help bridge the gap.

Problem: Inefficient Discharge Process

Patients who are ready for release frequently face delays owing to inadequate coordination among physicians, nurses, case managers, pharmacies, and even transportation providers. This causes bed bottlenecks, dissatisfied patients, and employee burnout.

How the Current Process Is Likely to Fail

- Outdated whiteboards containing inadequate information.
- Rounds occur at various times; therefore, updates are not real-time.
- Nurses pursuing physicians for discharge orders.
- Pharmacy is unaware that a patient is leaving home until the last minute.
- Transport is summoned too early (patient is not prepared) or too late.

How Collaboration Platforms Can Help

- Centralised discharge dashboard: Real-time status updates on each patient's tasks (medications available, transportation secured, etc.). Customisable notifications when something falls behind.
- Role-specific channels: A quick approach for the nurse to ask the physician if the order can be written, case management to discuss insurance difficulties, and so on, without playing phone tag.
- Automated notifications: The pharmacy is notified the instant the order is written. Transport is only notified when the patient is completely prepared.
- Integration potential: If the platform could retrieve estimated lengths of stay from the EHR, it would be even more useful for resource planning.

Incentivising Adoption

- The pain is real. Calculate current delays. How many hours have beds been occupied by patients who should have gone home? How much time does staff waste on phone calls?
- Physician focus: Showing doctors how the platform helps them get out the door sooner at the conclusion of a long day is more appealing than simply mentioning "efficiency."
- Nursing empowerment: Nurses frequently take the brunt of frustrated patients. Job satisfaction rises when employees have a tool that allows them to resolve delays in advance.
- Early adopters as champions: The transport worker boasting about how the new warnings cut down on unnecessary trips increases peer-to-peer buy-in.

Important Caveat

The platform cannot fix all problems on its own. The discharge procedure itself most certainly requires modification; the application simply facilitates communication around that better process.

Let's look at another scenario of the obstacles of disseminating research findings across a major healthcare system.

Problem: Siloed Research Efforts and Knowledge Dissemination

Even throughout huge organisations, research projects can become isolated. This leads to the following:

- Duplication of effort: Teams may be working on comparable challenges without knowing each other's progress.
- Missed collaboration opportunities: Researchers with complementary skills may never connect, limiting innovation.

■ Slow translation into practice: While breakthroughs are published in journals, front-line physicians are often ignorant of novel treatment alternatives or best practices that could improve care.

How Collaboration Platforms Can Help

■ The Research Project Directory serves as a searchable hub for ongoing and completed studies, as well as clear contact information for leads.
■ Discussion forums allow researchers to ask questions, receive comments on methodology, and connect with potential colleagues outside of their own department.
■ Pre-publication sharing: In a secure environment, findings can be shared for early feedback, potentially speeding up the development process.
■ Knowledge repository: Grant proposals, white papers, and other materials are organised and accessible, eliminating the need to reinvent the wheel for each initiative.
■ Integration with clinical systems: If practical, a method to notify physicians when a study finding is directly relevant to the patients they are seeing.

Incentivising Adoption

■ Focus on finding funding: Researchers are constantly searching for funds. The tool becomes a place to locate internal collaborators who can help strengthen apps.
■ Make them look good. A public-facing side of the platform that highlights the organisation's research can be utilised for recruitment, donor outreach, and so on. Researchers get recognition beyond their field.
■ The speed factor: Emphasise how the platform speeds up the process of getting answers to protocol queries, accessing specialised equipment within the system, and so on, compared to the previous method of relying on people they know.
■ Physician-researcher bridge: Busy clinicians are unlikely to review study results on their own. Facilitate Q&A sessions or concise recaps based on immediate practice consequences.

Challenges to consider

■ Intellectual property concerns: Researchers may be reluctant to share unpublished findings. Clear guidelines and potentially tiered access levels are required.
■ Data standardisation: If the goal is to aggregate findings for broader analyses, convincing researchers to utilise similar data formats is difficult.
■ Keep it alive: A static repository will not function. Needs dedicated community management, possibly with some gamification of contributions.

ADVANCED TOPICS AND CASE STUDIES

Chapter 8

Scaling Agile in Healthcare

Frameworks for Scaling Agile in Larger or Multi-Team Healthcare Projects

Scaling agile approaches in the context of big, complex healthcare projects necessitates frameworks that provide structure while retaining the flexibility and responsiveness that agile brings. Here's an outline of key frameworks and how they could be applied to healthcare:

Popular Scaling Frameworks

- Scrum of Scrums (SoS): Coordinates several scrum teams working on related areas of a project. Key roles include the chief product owner (who gives a high-level vision) and representatives from each scrum team who meet on a regular basis to handle dependencies.
- Scaled Agile Framework (SAFe®): A highly organised framework with many layers (team, programme, and portfolio) that aligns strategy and execution. Emphasises numerous release trains to ensure consistent delivery.
- Large-Scale Scrum (LeSS) aims to keep basic scrum principles even in huge projects. Instead of individual team deliverables, emphasis is placed on a single product backlog, cross-functional teams, and an overarching product focus.
- Disciplined Agile Delivery (DAD) is a flexible framework that enables teams to modify their process choices based on context. Prefers a "goal-driven" approach above prescriptive methods.

Tailoring for Healthcare Projects

- Regulation as a backdrop: SoS may be appropriate for an EHR implementation, in which sub-teams collaborate with the chief product owner to ensure that all modules meet regulatory requirements.
- Risk management isn't optional. SAFe's emphasis on predictability and release trains may be effective for projects that pose major patient safety risks and require constant monitoring and regular iterations.

DOI: 10.4324/9781032688435-11

- Embrace hybrid approaches: A large project may use LeSS concepts at the team level while incorporating some SoS structure for inter-team coordination.
- Do not forget DSDM: These scaling frameworks give methods for managing work inside DSDM's larger project structure (foundations, feasibility, etc.).

Key Considerations for Healthcare Projects

- The patient is the "why": Scaling should not create a chasm between those who are directly constructing the solution and the ultimate aim of better care. Find strategies to keep that connection strong.
- Clinical involvement at all levels: They must participate in the scaling process, either as representatives (as in SoS) or as members of cross-functional LeSS teams.
- Vendor relationships as dependencies: The framework must accommodate external vendors, who may not be as agile as internal teams.
- Start small and scale strategically. Do not attempt to develop a full-fledged, sophisticated scaling architecture from day one. Allow the project's needs to determine scaling decisions.

Example: Scaling for a Multi-Site Clinical Trial

The goal is to manage trials efficiently, ensure data integrity, and provide real-time insights across numerous geographically distributed sites.

Potential framework: A hybrid approach may be preferable.

- LeSS-style squads at each site: Responsible for duties under their authority (recruitment, follow-up, etc.).
- SAFe-inspired release train: To ensure that data standardisation, reporting, and protocol updates are rolled out consistently across all locations.
- DAD's flexibility: Allows for some customisation, as unexpected regulatory impediments may differ depending on locale.

Let's look at how scaling agile frameworks might help design a patient-centred AI diagnostic tool, as well as the specific hurdles to anticipate.

Project Considerations: Creating a Patient-Centred AI Diagnostic Tool

- Data diversity: In order to avoid bias and assure accuracy across varied patient populations, the algorithm must be trained on a big, representative data set.
- Regulatory scrutiny: The approval process (FDA or comparable) will be demanding. Documentation and validation processes must be included from the beginning.
- Clinician trust: Adoption depends on physicians knowing how the AI makes judgements and having confidence in its output as a decision support tool rather than a replacement for clinical judgement.
- Iterative by nature, the model will evolve as it encounters fresh data. Development and deployment cannot be "one and done" processes.

Potential Scaling Framework Elements

- LeSS for core development: Cross-functional teams of data scientists, developers, and clinical subject matter experts enable tight feedback loops and avoid the "throw it over the wall to IT" mindset.
- SoS for coordination: Sub-teams could work on data sourcing, UI/UX for the clinician interface, and the regulatory submission procedure. Syncing on a regular basis is vital.
- SAFe-inspired predictability: Release trains could be linked to model upgrades and rigorous validation. This enables progress, even though the final product may take years to be ready for public usage.
- DAD's goal-driven approach: Strict adherence to a single framework may be a disadvantage. The team requires the flexibility to change their procedure in response to evolving regulatory guidelines in the AI field.

Potential Drawbacks and Mitigations

- Data bottlenecks: If data sourcing and cleansing are done independently of development, the AI team will be delayed. Consider implementing a shared data platform or including data professionals in the development teams.
- The "explainability" problem: If the AI is a black box, it cannot be trusted. Involve visualisation experts early in the UI design process to ensure that the tool's reasoning is understandable to doctors.
- Premature scaling: Before you worry about enormous data sets and multi-team dynamics, be sure the basic model works on a small scale.
- Losing the patient voice: Involve patient representatives in user testing and feedback loops to ensure that the tool meets their needs and simplifies the diagnostic journey, rather than only providing technical accuracy.

Important Note

The technology is only half the battle. Change management, both during development (getting clinicians to help train the model) and deployment, is likely to be a separate project from the technical workstreams.

Let's look at the obstacles and concerns for scaling the implementation of a telehealth platform across many clinical settings. Then, we'll quickly discuss how to solve change management challenges unique to AI projects.

Scaling Telehealth Platform Rollout: A Balancing Act

Telehealth has enormous promise for improving access to care, but a successful large-scale implementation must take into account the distinct needs of diverse settings:

- Urban versus rural: Technology infrastructure may be a challenge in rural places. The platform must be user-friendly for patients with low technical knowledge.
- Specialty versus primary care: Dermatology may require high-resolution video consultations, whereas primary care may want rapid check-ins. The platform should be adaptive to various consultation styles.

■ Socioeconomic disparities: Not everyone has access to a dependable internet connection or device. The platform may require a phone-based option or low-bandwidth functionality.

Key Considerations for Different Settings

■ Pilot programmes: Begin small by evaluating the platform in a few clinics with varying characteristics. Before proceeding with full-scale implementation, refine depending on user input.
■ Phased rollout: Prioritise critical functions for the initial launch, then gradually add functionalities based on user demands and early adopter feedback.
■ Training and support: Clinicians, personnel, and patients all require platform usage, troubleshooting, and data security procedures. Multilingual support may be critical.
■ Flexibility and customisation: To accommodate changes in practice settings, the platform should allow for some customisation of workflows or appointment kinds.

Addressing Change Management Challenges in AI Projects

Building trust in AI, particularly in healthcare, necessitates a clearly defined change management plan. Here are a few early approaches:

■ Focus on transparency: Do not present AI as a panacea. Explain its operation, limits, and how technology complements clinical experience.
■ Involve clinicians early and often: Engage them in defining use cases, testing prototypes, and providing feedback. They will be advocates for the technology if they perceive it benefiting patient care.
■ Addressing biases head-on: Recognise that AI models might inherit biases from the data on which they are trained. Proactive steps to mitigate this are critical.
■ Start small and showcase values: Choose a low-risk region to illustrate AI's efficacy. A successful pilot can generate impetus for widespread adoption.

Remember, change management is a constant effort. As the platform grows, be prepared to address problems, provide continuing support, and adjust the technology in response to user feedback.

Maintaining Agility and Flexibility in Complex Healthcare Systems

Let's look at how healthcare organisations can remain agile despite the field's inherent difficulties.

Complex Healthcare Systems: The Challenge of Agility

■ Regulations and compliance: Rigid requirements and extensive documentation processes can seem at odds with agile's emphasis on quick iteration and adaptability to change.
■ Legacy systems: Outdated technology infrastructure and a hodgepodge of heterogeneous systems generate bottlenecks that stifle innovation. Integrating with them is difficult.

- Siloed departments: Cross-functional communication is essential for agility, but engrained departmental hierarchies, competing objectives, and possible turf wars all inhibit progress.
- Risk aversion: While sensible in healthcare, an overemphasis on avoiding mistakes can inhibit innovation and the "fail fast, learn fast" approach that agile values.
- External disruptors: The healthcare landscape is changing rapidly. Pandemic reactions, changing payment patterns, and new technologies necessitate agility that legacy processes were not designed for.

Strategies for Developing Agility

- Hybrid is your friend: Do not impose a one-size-fits-all agile strategy. Some projects may require the structure of DSDM paired with scrum execution. Others might benefit from kanban's flow-based strategy.
- Modular systems and open standards: Wherever practical, shift away from monolithic systems and towards smaller, interoperable systems with plug-and-play functionality. This allows for targeted improvements rather than a complete redesign.
- Focus on results, not rigid processes: A project that is delayed due to perfectly following a plan is considered a failure if it no longer fits the actual need. Accountability is based on delivering value rather than simply following steps.
- Dedicated "innovation zones": Establish areas within the organisation where risk tolerance is increased and regulatory requirements are reduced (within reason!). Small-scale experimentation can provide viable solutions for widespread implementation.
- Culture is key: Leadership must promote agility as a strategic aim, not just a technology trend. This includes:
  - Tolerance for failure as part of the learning process.
  - Celebrating cross-functional successes.
  - Investing in training employees to accept iterative attitudes.

Adapting in Real Time: Examples

- COVID-19 response: Organisations who needed to quickly deploy telehealth or triage policies couldn't wait for standard, lengthy process cycles. Agile methodologies were implemented out of need.
- AI development: Rather than a large initial requirements phase, teams may focus on iteratively constructing and evaluating the AI model with limited capabilities. This keeps them open to input and reduces the possibility of developing a flawless solution for the incorrect problem.
- Cloud-based solutions: Using cloud services for non-critical operations can reduce the IT burden by allowing teams to quickly set up development environments and experiment with new technology without requiring substantial infrastructure upgrades.

Important Notes

- This is a mindset shift: Agile is more than simply tooling and sprint schedules; it is about accepting change as a constant in healthcare.
- Do not confuse agility with chaos. Agile does not imply a lack of documentation or disregard for safety measures. It is about striking the appropriate balance for specific projects within the framework of the larger healthcare system.

Fostering Agility in Complex Healthcare Organisations: A Sectoral Breakdown

Large healthcare systems, pharmaceutical corporations, and public health agencies all play important roles in healthcare delivery, but each has unique problems when it comes to remaining agile in a complex and ever-changing environment. Here's a description of their individual challenges and how agile principles might be applied to their contexts:

Large Hospital System

Challenges include bureaucracy and compliance, which can impede decision-making and iterative processes.

- Siloed departments: Fragmented communication and competitiveness across departments can inhibit cross-functional collaboration, which is critical for agile.
- Legacy infrastructure: Outdated IT systems might make it difficult to integrate new technology and implement agile practices.

Fostering Agility

- Focus on value streams: Identify care pathways and connect them to agile workflows to simplify operations and improve patient flow.
- Centres of excellence: Establish dedicated units focusing on specific areas (e.g., telehealth) to test agile approaches and share findings with the larger system.
- Empowerment and ownership: Allow frontline employees more authority in decision-making and problem-solving within well-defined boundaries.

Pharmaceutical Companies

Challenges include lengthy and rigid drug discovery, testing, and approval processes, which can slow down innovation.

- Risk aversion: The high stakes of drug development might lead to an overemphasis on safety and a reluctance to try new things.
- Global operations: Coordinating research and development across multiple geographical regions with varied regulations increases complexity.

Fostering Agility

- Fail fast culture: Encourage early experimentation and take calculated risks, learning from mistakes to speed up drug development.
- Digital transformation: Use data analytics, artificial intelligence, and cloud-based solutions to simplify research operations and clinical trials.
- Modular R&D: Divide R&D processes into smaller, modular components to enable concurrent research and faster iteration.

Public Health Agencies

Challenges in public health include responding rapidly to emerging infectious diseases and adapting to changing environments.

- Limited resources: Budget limits and manpower shortages might make it difficult to integrate new technologies or scale up quickly.
- Collaboration across jurisdictions: Effective public health solutions frequently include collaboration between local, regional, and national authorities, which can be difficult.

Fostering Agility

- Data-driven decision making: Use real-time data analytics to detect outbreaks and trends, informing targeted responses.
- Partnerships and collaboration: Develop strong working partnerships with other public health agencies, healthcare providers, and community organisations to ensure a coordinated response.
- Scenario planning and simulations: Practice probable public health emergencies on a regular basis to fine-tune response strategies and develop a preparation culture.

Actionable Insights

Understanding these distinct difficulties allows us to design agile techniques to each sector.

- Large hospital systems: Concentrate on optimising internal processes and empowering employees to improve patient flow and service delivery.
- Pharmaceutical companies: Take calculated risks and use technology to accelerate medication development in a safe and ethical environment.
- Public health agencies should prioritise data analysis and collaboration in order to efficiently respond to shifting risks and maximise resource utilisation.

Remember that agility is not a one-size-fits-all answer. The goal is to tailor agile concepts to the unique environment and difficulties faced by each healthcare organisation. Healthcare institutions may become more sensitive and flexible to patients' and public health's ever-changing requirements by cultivating an innovative, collaborative, and continuous learning culture.

Chapter 9

Managing Risks and Compliance in Healthcare Projects

Identifying and Mitigating Risks Specific to Healthcare Projects

Let us now get into the essential work of identifying and managing the risks that are inherent in healthcare projects.

Identifying and Mitigating Risks for Healthcare Projects

While all initiatives involve some risk, healthcare projects have heightened stakes due to the potential for a direct influence on patient safety and well-being. Here are the main risk categories and mitigation strategies:

Patient Safety and Data Security

Risks:

- Medical errors occur when technology fails or data are entered incorrectly.
- Data breaches jeopardise patient privacy and violate HIPAA regulations.
- System failures or downtime can affect vital care delivery operations.

Mitigation strategy:

- Health IT solutions are rigorously tested and validated using user scenarios that are representative of clinical practice.
- Multilayered cybersecurity protections (encryption, access controls, and effective incident response strategies).

DOI: 10.4324/9781032688435-12

- Redundant systems and backup procedures are used to minimise interruption in the event of an outage.
- Patient involvement in co-designing systems aids in identifying potential faults from their perspective.

Regulatory Compliance

Risks:

- Changes in legislation throughout a protracted project can result in costly rework and probable delays.
- Noncompliance can result in fines, reputational damage, or even the suspension of activities.
- It is difficult to navigate many regulatory organisations (FDA, local health departments, etc.) with overlapping regulations.

Mitigation strategy:

- Dedicated compliance expert integrated within the project team, preferably with domain-specific knowledge.
- Proactive engagement with regulatory organisations, particularly for initiatives involving emerging technologies or undiscovered territory.
- "Build for compliance" is a philosophy, not an afterthought. Documentation must show adherence from day one.
- Scenario-based testing to check that the solution is consistent with various interpretations of legislation.

Clinical Adoption and Workflow Disruption

Risks:

- Clinicians' resistance to change causes underutilisation or outright rejection of new systems.
- Poorly designed workflows that put additional strain on employees, perhaps introducing new dangers.
- Negative impact on the patient experience, leading to irritation and discontent.

Mitigation strategy:

- Early and continued clinician engagement across all project phases (preferably as part of the core team rather than as testers at the end).
- Phased rollout with comprehensive training and support for various user groups, tailored to their individual requirements.
- Iteration based on feedback, with the willingness to alter workflows even after launch.
- Celebrate successes openly – when a new tool prevents an error or increases efficiency, spread the word.

Ethical Considerations

Risks:

- AI algorithms reinforce or exacerbate existing biases in healthcare delivery.
- The unintended repercussions of emerging technologies for vulnerable patient populations.
- Erosion of patient confidence and privacy in the name of innovation.

Mitigation strategy:

- Diverse data sets for training AI algorithms that encourage justice.
- Ethical review boards or separate responsibilities within the project team to investigate potential unintended consequences.
- Transparency regarding data utilisation and technological restrictions for both patients and professionals.
- Framework for continued monitoring and addressing ethical concerns after the first project is completed.

Healthcare-Specific Risk Management Tools

- Failure mode and effects analysis (FMEA) is a proactive, process-focused technique for identifying probable failure locations and their implications. This is especially crucial in healthcare, where failure can have serious implications.
- Clinical risk assessments: Use clinical skills to identify dangers that non-healthcare IT project members may overlook.
- Patient and community engagement: Feedback tools (surveys, focus groups) give information about perceived hazards from the user's perspective.

Let's look at the specific hazards connected with two different types of healthcare projects and propose mitigation techniques.

Project 1: Wearable Device Development (e.g., A Smartwatch for Blood Glucose Monitoring)

- **Accuracy and reliability risks**: The gadget must collect trustworthy data, and the algorithms must accurately interpret it. Failure here could result in a dangerous misdiagnosis and incorrect treatment.
    - **Mitigation**: Extensive testing in a variety of real-world scenarios, not simply controlled lab environments. Clinical trials will be conducted to validate against the existing gold-standard measuring methodologies.
- **Data privacy risks**: Highly sensitive health information is obtained. Breaches have major ramifications that extend beyond conventional consumer wearables.
    - **Mitigation**: Security by design. Encryption, minimum data gathering, and user clarity about what information is saved and how it is utilised.
- **Adoption and behavioural change risks**: Will users constantly wear the device? Will they comprehend how to act on the information? Even the best device fails if it sits in a drawer.
    - **Mitigation**: Human-centred design for comfort and ease of usage. Integration with existing care routines provides clinicians with meaningful insights rather than just raw data dumps.
- **Regulatory risks**: The approval process for medical wearables is complex. Delays or unexpected requirements may disrupt the project schedule.
    - **Mitigation**: Early consultation with the FDA (or a comparable agency). A specialised regulatory specialist on the project team is essential.

Project 2: Public Health Campaign (e.g., Promoting HPV Vaccination in Teenagers)

- **Misinformation risks**: This topic is riddled with disinformation. The marketing may unwittingly perpetuate misconceptions or cause outrage.
  - **Mitigation**: Conducting pre-test messaging with focus groups from the target population. Partnering with trusted community voices to serve as ambassadors rather than merely government-created products.
- **Accessibility risks**: Does the marketing reach everyone? Materials in the wrong language, or a reliance on internet connectivity, may exclude individuals in greatest need of the information.
  - **Mitigation** strategies include a multi-channel strategy (schools, clinics, and community centres), as well as translation services. Consider combining low-tech solutions (posters at doctors' offices) with social media strategies.
- **Measuring impact risk**: Success is more difficult to quantify than a technical project. Was the increase in vaccination rates due to the campaign or other factors?
  - **Mitigation**: Gather baseline data before launching. If possible, include a control group (same demographics but no campaign exposure) for comparison. Track not only vaccines but also proxy measures (appointments, website visits) to gain a comprehensive picture of impact.
- **Sustainability risks**: A single shove disappears from recollection. Is the campaign intended to be an ongoing effort with resources to update materials as needed?
  - **Mitigation**: Increase capacity within community organisations to continue the task, rather than relying exclusively on the health department's bandwidth.

Important Notes

- Projects frequently involve overlapping hazards. A badly designed wearable interface raises patient safety concerns and reduces adoption. Consider the interaction of risk factors.
- Risk is not eliminated; it is managed. Being aware of the risks allows for pre-emptive measures, which improves the project's chances of success even in a hostile healthcare environment.

Navigating Healthcare Regulations and Ensuring Compliance (e.g., HIPAA, GDPR, Local Regulations)

Navigating the complicated jungle of healthcare laws is critical for project success and protecting patient data. Let's look at techniques for complying with frameworks like HIPAA, General Data Protection Regulation (GDPR), and various local legislation.

Navigating Healthcare Regulations: Ensuring Compliance

1. **Understand the regulatory landscape**: Beyond HIPAA. HIPAA is the baseline in the United States, although other requirements may apply depending on the complexity of the project.
   - FDA laws govern medical equipment and software.
   - Substance abuse records are protected under 42 CFR Part 2.
   - State-specific privacy regulations that may be much harsher than HIPAA.

Global considerations: GDPR applies if you handle data from EU residents. Similar legislation is evolving in other areas.

Do not rely solely on the IT team: Clinicians, researchers, and others may interact with systems in ways that have unforeseen compliance ramifications. Broad comprehension is required.

2. **"Privacy by design" approach** includes built-in compliance. Consider how sensitive health data will be collected, stored, and used from the start of the project. Retrofitting solutions for compliance is expensive and hazardous.

   Minimise data collection: Do you really require the patient's complete address, or is a zip code sufficient? Less data implies lower danger of a compromise.

   Transparency is key. Clear, patient-friendly explanations of how their information is utilised foster confidence. This is frequently a regulatory obligation, but it is also excellent practice for the adoption of new technologies.

3. **Dedicated compliance expertise**

   The right role: A healthcare privacy and security specialist should be integrated into the project team. Depending on the project's complexity, this could be a full-time position or a consultant brought in during vital stages.

   More than checklists: They require a seat at the table throughout the design phase, rather than merely examining paperwork at the end. Their feedback might assist avoid solutions that are technically possible but result in compliance headaches.

4. **Vendor management**

   Your responsibility and their data: If the project includes third-party providers (cloud hosting, etc.), their compliance policies are important. Ensure that contracts include provisions for data handling, breach notification, and liability.

   Audits and certification: Ask for proof System and Organization Controls (SOC) 2 reports, for example), rather than relying just on the sales presentation. Reputation counts, but make sure they have the proper systems in place to protect healthcare data.

5. **Staying current**: Regulations are not static; new interpretations of current laws, revisions in response to growing technological dangers, and wholly new laws must all be watched.

   Training and awareness: Compliance should not be a once-a-year click-through training for employees. This is kept in mind through brief, regular updates that include real-world examples pertinent to their work.

Additional Considerations

De-identification: Proper de-identification techniques are critical while conducting research or sharing data sets with partners. Data that are labelled as "anonymised" are rarely genuinely anonymous.

Incident response planning: Breaches will occur at some point. Having a well-defined response plan (notification of affected patients, forensics, etc.) reduces harm while demonstrating that the organisation takes compliance seriously.

Let us examine the regulatory challenges at various stages of development for two healthcare project categories with significant regulatory implications:

Project 1: AI Diagnostic Tool (Example: Algorithm for Analysing Radiological Imaging)

CONCEPTUAL STAGE

- FDA classification: Is the instrument designed to supplement a clinician's diagnosis or provide an independent diagnosis? This determines the extent of regulatory inspection.
- Data bias: Will the algorithm be based on existing historical data? Consider whether the data contains biases, which the AI will subsequently mirror. Plans for dealing with this issue must be in place from the beginning.

- Intellectual property: Who owns the algorithm if it was developed in collaboration with a university? Clear agreements made early minimise costly conflicts later.

GATHERING DATA STAGE

- De-identification: Even if utilised to train the AI, patient data must be thoroughly de-identified. Consider more stringent rules than HIPAA's minimum.
- Consent: Was the original data obtained for a reason that is relevant to its current application in AI development? Older consent forms may not cover this.
- International data: Data sets collected outside of the United States may be subject to different privacy legislation that govern their use.

DEPLOYMENT STAGE

- FDA approval: Extensive research and clinical trials will be required, particularly for higher-risk gadgets that perform their own diagnostics.
- Explainability: Can the AI's "decision" be explained in a way that clinicians can understand? Black boxes, no matter how accurate, will be rejected.
- Ongoing monitoring: The AI is likely to evolve. Processes are required for retraining the model on new data to ensure its safety and effectiveness.

Project 2: Telehealth Platform (Example: Focusing on Mental Health Treatments)

CONCEPTUAL STAGE

- Can therapists licenced in one state treat patients across state borders using the platform? Regulations vary greatly.
- Data security: While all telemedicine must be HIPAA compliant, mental health notes frequently include additional legal safeguards. More stringent encryption requirements may be required.
- Malpractice coverage: Does a provider's current insurance cover telehealth? What if anything is overlooked that should have been picked up in person?

GATHERING DATA STAGE

- International considerations: If you want to offer services all over the world, GDPR and other privacy requirements apply. The platform will need to change depending on the patient's placement.
- Patient identity verification: How does the platform ensure that the patient is who they claim to be? This lowers the possibility of fraud, which is especially crucial for controlled substance prescriptions.

DEPLOYMENT STAGE

- Asynchronous services: Are any consultations conducted via text or saved messages? Regulations governing the documentation of those contacts may exist.
- Crisis response: What is the protocol if a patient displays suicidal thoughts on the platform? The team requires clear escalation methods that account for the limits of remote care.
- Interoperability: Will telehealth visit notes seamlessly link with the patient's EHR? This affects care continuity.

IMPORTANT REMINDERS

- Regulations are continually developing. Do not presume that what was true last year is still true now.
- "Agile" does not imply abandoning compliance. The technique can be flexible, but patient safety is not negotiable.

Data Security Considerations in Agile Healthcare Projects

Strong data security measures are critical in healthcare operations that rely on sensitive patient data. Let's look at how agile practices may be used to prioritise security at all stages.

Data Security Considerations for Agile Healthcare Projects

1. **Security from the beginning, not an afterthought**

    Shift-left mindset: Include security specialists early in architecture discussions and sprint planning. This avoids costly rework if problems arise later.

    Conduct regular **threat modelling** exercises to identify potential weaknesses and develop proactive countermeasures. Consider both system flaws and user behaviour concerns (e.g., clicking phishing links).

    Secure coding practices: Train developers on secure coding approaches particular to the technology utilised (e.g., defending against SQL injection). Include security-focused testing in the "definition of done."

2. **Protecting data throughout its lifecycle**

    At rest: Strong encryption for data stored in databases, systems, or even individual devices that contain sensitive information.

    In transit: Secure transmission methods Transport Layer Security (TLS), particularly for data transiting between systems not under the organisation's direct control.

    In use: Base data access on user roles and the specific task at hand. Time-limited access decreases the possibility of misuse.

3. **Privacy by design**

    Data minimisation: Does the solution need to acquire all patient data? The fewer data you have, the less likely it will be revealed in a breach.

    User consent: Provide clear, patient-facing explanations of how data are handled and obtained. Opt-in models, when available, foster confidence.

    De-identification where possible: Data sets used for analytics or AI training may not require full patient identifiers. Proper de-identification techniques are critical, and the danger of re-identification must be constantly monitored.

4. **Access controls and auditing**

    Role-based permissions. Nurses, physicians, administrators, and other personnel should have varying levels of data access. Regular assessments ensure that these permissions remain appropriate as job functions shift.

    Robust logging: Detailed logs of who accessed what data, when, and why act as a deterrent and are required for incident investigations.

    Avoid shared accounts. Individual logins are essential for accountability. This can be more challenging in healthcare settings with shift changes, but it must be balanced with clinical workflow.

5. **Vendor management**

    Inspect their security: If a third party handles patient data (cloud hosting, for example), you are responsible for their security. Don't just believe certifications; ask for thorough documentation of their methods.

    Clear contracts: Determine breach notification timescales, data handling limits, and responsibility. This lowers risks and encourages vendors to take security seriously.

Agile Adaptation

- Security user stories: Include tasks such "As a patient, I want to be notified if any unauthorised access to my data is detected," as well as functional needs.
- Short feedback loops: Conduct regular penetration tests and use vulnerability scanning technologies to swiftly discover and address security vulnerabilities as the project progresses.
- Security champions: Have a team member committed to security. This ensures that everyone is aware rather than relying entirely on an external team.

Let's break down the specific security challenges and mitigation options for each healthcare project scenario you mentioned.

Scenario #1: Wearable Device

- **Data in motion**: Data transmission from the device to the cloud (often via a user's smartphone) is a common target for interception.
    - **Mitigation** includes strong encryption protocols (TLS), regular security fixes for the wearable's firmware, and training users not to sync on unprotected public Wi-Fi networks.
- **The device itself**: If the wearable keeps data locally before syncing, there is a vulnerability. Lost or stolen gadgets may allow unauthorised access.
    - **Mitigation** measures include automatic data erasure following successful sync, re-authentication after a period **of** inactivity, and remote wipe functionality if the device is reported lost.
- **Cloud storage**: Reputable cloud providers offer strong security, but misconfiguration on your end may expose data.
    - **Mitigation**: Implement strict access controls inside the cloud environment, conduct frequent security audits, and consider encryption even for data at rest in your cloud storage.
- **Physician access**: Is the doctor able to examine data via a secure portal, or are reports emailed? Your risk is based on the clinician's weaknesses.
    - **Mitigation** measures include two-factor authentication for the portal, avoiding emailed reports if possible, and user education for physicians to ensure that sensitive data is not downloaded to insecure computers, amongst other things.

Scenario #2: Research Data Set

- **De-identification** can be difficult because simply removing names and addresses is insufficient. An unusual condition, when combined with a zip code and age, can often identify someone.
    - **Mitigation**: Techniques such as data suppression (removing specific fields), generalisation (age ranges rather than specific birthdays), and introducing a modest amount of "noise" to the data can help.
- **The risk of re-identification**: Particularly when paired with other data sets. A researcher with malicious intent could potentially reveal persons' identities.
    - **Mitigation**: Strict access controls to the data set, which may require researchers to work in a protected data enclave where it cannot be easily downloaded. Contracts that define the repercussions for misuse are also deterrents.
- **Utility versus privacy**: A heavily de-identified data set may not be relevant for some research.
    - Tiered access levels could be a solution. Only a tiny internal staff receives fully identified data. Collaborators can access more de-identified versions, as well as obfuscated data for large-scale, open sharing.

Scenario #3: AI Development

- **"Anonymised" is not always**: Can seemingly innocuous data from a vast data set, when processed by an AI algorithm, be linked back to an individual?
  - **Mitigation**: Differential privacy techniques can introduce noise in a way that preserves general statistical trends while protecting specific data points. This area of research is rapidly evolving.
- **The AI model itself**: Could someone reverse engineer the model to reveal information about the patients it was trained on?
  - **Mitigation**: Federated learning, which trains on data spread across numerous universities rather than a single central data set, can lessen this risk.
- **Data drift**: As AI is deployed in production, patient populations or demographics may shift, making the model less accurate and possibly revealing biases in the initial training data.
  - **Mitigation**: Continuous performance monitoring is required, together with defined procedures for retraining and reapproval when accuracy thresholds are no longer fulfilled.

Important note: Data security is never a "solved" issue. Healthcare personnel must stay up to date on the latest threat vectors and best practices through ongoing training and knowledge exchange.

Chapter 10

Fifteen Case Studies

Examples of Healthcare Project Case Studies Managed Using DSDM and Agile

Let's look at some healthcare project case studies and see how DSDM and agile approaches may provide structure and flexibility to ensure success (Table 10.1).

Project 1: Patient Engagement Portal Development

Problem: A hospital aims to improve customer happiness while also reducing administrative burdens by allowing online appointment scheduling, bill payment, and access to test results.

DSDM approach:
  - Feasibility/foundations: Evaluate existing systems, identify regulatory/security challenges, and perform extensive user research (patients, clinicians, billing staff) to understand the needs of various user groups.
  - Timeboxing: Divide development into modules: core (scheduling, seeing basic results) and add-ons (secure messaging with providers, prescription refill requests).
  - Prioritisation: Must-haves for launch, with an ongoing backlog of future enhancements based on user data.
Agile approach:
  - Cross-functional team: Developers, UI/UX experts, clinical SMEs, and, most importantly, patient reps to provide feedback.
  - Sprints: Prioritise delivering functioning versions of certain features for testing.
  - User stories: "As a patient with limited mobility, I want to be able to schedule a follow-up appointment without calling."

Project 2: AI-Assisted Radiology Tool

Problem: Radiologists are overloaded, causing delays and the possibility of missed diagnoses. A tool could help with the initial examination of photos, identifying regions for further review.

DSDM approach:
  - Feasibility/foundations: It is critical to understand what the tool cannot accomplish (give diagnoses independently) in order to manage expectations and meet regulatory issues.

DOI: 10.4324/9781032688435-13

Table 10.1 List of Healthcare Projects

Project Number	Project Title	Technology Focus	Target User	Complexity	Notes
1	Patient engagement portal development	Workflow optimisation	Patient/clinician	Small-medium	Balancing diverse user needs may require a mix of timeboxes and sprints
2	AI-assisted radiology tool	Clinical tools	Clinician	Large-scale	Regulatory hurdles, need for ongoing validation with new data sets
3	Redesigning a hospital unit workflow	Workflow optimisation	Clinician/staff	Small-medium	Process flaws may be deeper than tech fixes, change management is key
4	Disease outbreak tracking	Data management	Public health	Medium-large	Initial focus on speed, later iterations focused on data accuracy
5	National clinical data repository	Data management	Researchers	Large-scale	Governance is more of a hurdle than the tech, may need DSDM buy-in
6	Telehealth for underserved populations	Clinical tools	Patient	Small-medium	Requires "agile with empathy," social factors can't be an afterthought
7	Streamlining clinical trial processes	Workflow optimisation	Researchers	Medium-large	Inflexibility is the enemy, adapting as regulations and protocols shift
8	Remote patient monitoring (heart failure)	Clinical tools	Patient/clinician	Small-medium	Behavioural aspects are as crucial as the tech, device ergonomics matter
9	National adverse drug event reporting system	Data management	Clinician/public	Medium-large	Trust-building alongside usability, data alone won't drive adoption
10	Precision medicine initiative	Data management	Researchers	Transformational	Immense scientific and data challenges, needs long-term adaptable plan

(Continued)

Table 10.1 (Continued)

Project Number	Project Title	Technology Focus	Target User	Complexity	Notes
11	Mental health crisis response app	Clinical tools	Patient	Small-medium	Safety is paramount, needs clinician input even for a patient-facing tool
12	Supply chain optimisation for rural clinics	Workflow optimisation	Clinic staff	Small-medium	Localised solutions needed, tech is only part of the solution
13	Rehabilitation game design	Clinical tools	Patient/ clinician	Small-medium	Fun versus therapeutic is a delicate balance, needs ongoing rehab input
14	Blockchain for medical supply chain	Other	Industry-wide	Transformational	Regulatory unknowns, getting buy-in across a fragmented industry is key
15	Social determinants of health data platform	Data management	Multi-sector	Large-scale	Actionable data are vital, potential for both DSDM upfront and agile iterations based on usage patterns

- Timeboxing is the process of iterating over larger data sets and more complex images. Validation phases ensure that the AI remains accurate.
- Rigorous collaboration: Radiologists are major partners throughout the process, not just given tools at the end.

Agile approach:
- Data-driven development: The AI's performance will be limited by the data on which it is taught. An agile team structure enables rapid data set sourcing and cleaning.
- Explainability focus: Sprints targeted to building confidence with the radiologist by communicating the AI's "reasoning."
- Test, test, test: Use simulated and real-world scenarios using various data sets to detect bias early.

Project 3: Designing a Hospital Unit Workflow

Problem: Inefficiencies in a nursing unit cause bottlenecks, medication errors, and patient unhappiness. The root reason is not only technological but also process-related.

DSDM approach:
- Feasibility/foundations: Create a detailed map of present workflows. Don't assume everyone has the same idea of what's "broken." Identify fast wins and long-term solutions.
- Timeboxing: Perhaps a shift schedule modification can be evaluated in a single timebox alongside an iteration on a new medicine administration documentation system.
- Outcomes based: The emphasis on generating business value makes DSDM an excellent choice for process optimisation. Metrics are established beforehand (time to first dose of antibiotic, etc.).

Agile approach:
- Frontline staff are critical: Their insights are more useful than those of an outside consultant.
- Sprints for trial and error: Try a new rounding approach, gather feedback, then quickly modify for the next sprint.
- Accept imperfect solutions: An 80% improvement over a chaotic system is preferable to waiting indefinitely for perfection.

Project 4: Disease Outbreak Tracking

Problem: A public health department must quickly implement a system for tracking cases, identifying possible hotspots, and coordinating response operations to a new infectious disease outbreak.

DSDM approach:
- Minimal, yet crucial "foundations": Define critical data points, keeping in mind that requirements may change as knowledge of the condition grows. Determine the privacy versus public health data demands.
- Timeboxing with contingency: The initial implementation focuses on case reporting, with concurrent timeboxes planned for scenarios such as vaccine tracking, communication modules, and so on.
- Stakeholder input: Epidemiologists, doctors, lab professionals, and communication experts all need to have a say in building the system.

Agile approach:
- Flexible data model: As the outbreak proceeds, the system should be able to readily accommodate new fields or changes to case definitions.
- Short sprints and prioritised features: Dashboard visualisations for decision-making may be more important initially than detailed patient-level statistics.
- "Good enough" mentality: A system that is 85% correct and deploys rapidly is preferable to waiting for perfection as cases increase.

Project 5: The National Clinical Data Repository

Data silos impede research progress. A centralised repository could speed up research, but it presents significant logistical and governance issues.

> DSDM approach:
> – Before coding begins, a lengthy, in-depth procedure must be completed to map existing data sources, quality issues, legal impediments (cross-country variances if international), and stakeholder buy-in.
> – Incremental timeboxing: Perhaps beginning with a specific disease region or a few sorts of data sets to test the concept before a large-scale rollout.
> – Governance structure: DSDM can give a structure for making transparent decisions and resolving disagreements.
>
> Agile approach:
> – Standardisation sprints: Concentrate on data dictionaries, ontologies, and so on, while acknowledging that perfection is the enemy of progress.
> – Emphasis on user needs: Researchers must help define what a viable repository interface should look like.
> – Security by design: Iterations focused on anonymisation techniques and attack simulations.

Project 6: Telehealth for Underserved Populations

Problem: Socioeconomic variables impede healthcare access. A telehealth programme must handle not only technological issues, but also language difficulties, health literacy, and a lack of patient technology expertise.

> DSDM approach:
> – Foundations are social: A thorough grasp of the target population must drive requirements, rather than assuming a one-size-fits-all solution.
> – Deployment timeboxing: Consider starting with certain clinics that already have strong relationships to the community, allowing for lessons learned before a larger deployment.
> – Prioritising help: Initially, a tech-forward patient portal may be a "won't have" in favour of phone-based help.
>
> Agile approach:
> – The story of empathy: "As a grandmother with limited English who gets confused by medical terms, I want to be able to…"
> – Feedback loops: Thorough tracking of not only whether patients attended the appointment but also the quality of the engagement, including if it met their needs.
> – Iteration on outreach: Attempted text reminders but failed? Sprint to investigate alternate communication channels.

Project 7: Streamline Clinical Trial Processes

Problem: Trials are notoriously sluggish and cumbersome, with data collected on paper forms and manually entered into systems that have little integration.

> DSDM approach:
> – Assess the feasibility and foundations of research sites. Are they prepared to move away from paper? Determine the regulatory limits on what data can be acquired electronically.

- Timeboxing: Consider beginning with a less sophisticated sort of trial (patient survey-based) to gather expertise before moving on to multi-site, interventional pharmacological research.
- Prioritisation of data integrity: Features that reduce manual entry and improve data validation from the start are critical.

Agile approach:
- Co-design with sites: Research coordinators have firsthand experience of bottlenecks. Their feedback on the tools is critical to uptake.
- Sprints for integration: Collaborate with existing trial management providers to develop application programming interfaces (APIs) that ensure data flow between systems.
- Adapting to new requirements: As legislation or trial protocols change, the system must be flexible without requiring extensive rework.

Project 8: Remote Patient Monitoring (Heart Failure)

Problem: Frequent readmissions for heart failure are expensive and disruptive. Remote monitoring of weight, blood pressure, and other parameters could enable early management, but patient compliance is difficult to achieve.

DSDM approach:
- Beyond technology, is the target demographic comfortable with the devices? Are there any home care resources available when alerts are triggered?
- Timeboxing with behavioural focus: Perhaps the initial iteration is simply encouraging patients to take readings consistently, with subsequent additions of automated notifications to clinicians.
- Data isn't enough: Clear decision trees for the clinical team receiving the data are required to demonstrate value.

Agile approach:
- Iteration on device ergonomics: If an elderly patient population has difficulty with devices, feedback sprints for device design are recommended.
- Personalised communication: Experiment in sprints with alert frequency and approach to increase engagement and reduce false alarms.
- Gamification potential: Sprints that incorporate elements of achievement or light competitiveness may make the task less of a chore for patients.

Project 9: The National Adverse Drug Event Reporting System

Problem: Side effects are underreported, making it difficult to identify safety risks. A centralised system is required, but it faces trust and usability challenges.

DSDM approach:
- Thorough feasibility: How can we strike a compromise between ease of use and data that is thorough enough for analysis? What are the incentives for reporting?
- Timeboxing for confidence: The initial rollout may focus on clinicians, where data quality can be more tightly monitored, with public reporting added later.
- Transparency is essential: Provide clear explanations of how the data are used (and safeguarded) in conjunction with the reporting tool.

Agile approach:
- Sprints for user groups: The interface for a busy chemist should differ from that of a concerned patient.
- Collaboration with pharma: How can their current processes be integrated to reduce duplicative reporting?

- AI potential: Sprints focused on natural language processing to extract data from unstructured text fields and supplement coded information.

Project 10: Precision Medicine Initiative

Problem: Using genomic data to tailor treatment, yet present data are siloed and insufficiently scaled for robust insights.

DSDM approach:
- Extensive feasibility: Research institution stakeholder buy-in, ethical issues for data sharing, and overcoming the enormous technical challenges of varied data sets.
- Timeboxing by disease: Perhaps start with one type of disease to establish success before expanding to a larger catalogue.
- Governance overhaul: DSDM makes it easier to define a decision-making framework for data access and research proposal prioritisation.

Agile approach:
- Sprints for standardisation: Creating standard data formats and ontologies for gene variations.
- AI-focused teams: Dedicated sprints for developing algorithms to detect patterns and clinically actionable insights in data.
- Clinician-facing tools: Iterative development of bedside decision assistance tools based on complicated genetic data.

Project 11: Mental Health Crisis Response App

Problem: People in mental health crises frequently wind up in the ER or with police involvement. An app might offer information, self-help guides, and direct access to trained responders via chat or video.

DSDM approach:
- Safety features that allow for fast emergency escalation (connection with local 911 systems, location sharing) are prioritised.
- Timeboxing for triage: Using algorithms or a chatbot to determine severity and link people to the appropriate level of support.
- Foundations with experts: Psychologists and crisis responders must lead content creation, ensuring it is both helpful and does not escalate the problem.

Agile approach:
- Privacy-focused sprints include features for safe communication and data storage, as well as user-friendly explanations.
- Emphasis on user input: Mechanisms for in-the-moment and post-crisis input to improve the experience.
- Data for advocacy: Anonymised usage data could help lawmakers understand the demand for expanded mental health services.

Project 12: Supply Chain Optimisation for Rural Clinics

Problem: Unreliable supply chains cause pharmaceutical shortages and waste in resource-constrained areas.

DSDM approach:
- Mapping the mess: Identifying areas where breakdowns occur, such as antiquated inventory systems and unreliable transportation.

- Prioritisation based on impact: Perhaps resolving the "cold chain" issue for vaccinations is more important than developing an elaborate forecasting model.
- Timeboxing for localised solutions: Due to variances in geography and infrastructure, what works in one place may not work in another.

Agile approach:
- Frugal innovation: Sprints to test low-tech solutions (SMS-based inventory alerts) while also researching more complex technology.
- Data collection mechanisms: How can basic consumption and demand data be collected given the current constraints?
- Embrace local expertise: Clinic workers are aware of workarounds; the system needs to formalise and scale them.

Project 13: Rehabilitation Game Design

Problem: Rehabilitation following a stroke or injury can be time-consuming. Games could improve engagement, but commercially available ones are not therapeutically useful.

DSDM approach:
- Possibility with therapists: Determine which movements require recording and what form of feedback is most effective for recovery.
- Modular timeboxing: Divide the game into body areas (hand rehab, then balance-based) to allow for more concentrated development.

Agile approach:
- Sprints with patient feedback: Is the game fun? Motivating? Or does it feel like a chore cloaked in vibrant colours?
- Data collection focus: Can the game accurately record motion data for clinicians to evaluate and objectively track progression?
- Adaptive difficulty: Sprints to develop AI-lite difficulty modifications to avoid boredom and frustration.

Project 14: Blockchain for the Medical Supply Chain

Problem: Counterfeit pharmaceuticals and questionable provenance of key supplies pose considerable dangers, particularly in global supply networks.

DSDM approach:
- Extensive feasibility: Major challenges include the regulatory framework, blockchain computational costs, and gaining buy-in from a fragmented sector.
- Timeboxing with pilots: Begin with a single, high-value medicine or device type in a controlled network before attempting broader application.
- Focus on tangible benefits: DSDM emphasises showing value; therefore, track unambiguous indicators to justify the investment (decrease in recalls, for example).

Agile approach:
- UI/UX for diverse users: Sprints focused on making the interface useful for everyone from manufacturers to front-line chemists.
- Interoperability challenges: Iterative strategies to allow data entry from existing inventory systems to avoid duplicate effort.
- Adapting to new threats: Agile teams are well-equipped to respond to new sorts of fraud attempts by modifying ledger rules.

Project 15: The Social Determinants of Health Data Platform

Problem: Healthcare frequently focuses primarily on clinical concerns, ignoring how housing, poverty, and other variables influence outcomes. Data to address this exists; however, it is fragmented and incompatible.

DSDM approach:
- Stakeholder complexity: The foundations phase will necessitate input from public health agencies, social services, community groups, and healthcare professionals.
- Timeboxing by outcome: Consider prioritising one issue (asthma and home quality) to test the concept before expanding.
- Prioritisation of actionable data: Simply showing discrepancies is insufficient. The platform must enable targeted interventions.

Agile approach:
- Partnership sprints: Collaborate with existing community organisations who are likely already collecting some of this data.
- Dashboards can effectively communicate complicated insights that guide lobbying activities and resource allocation.
- Iteration on privacy: How to strike a balance between using individual data to inform care and safeguarding vulnerable people from further harm.

Lessons Learned and Best Practices

Let's make a table with essential lessons learned and best practices specific to the 15 projects (Table 10.2).

Let's break down Projects 1–15 to highlight those concrete lessons and tie them to DSDM and agile techniques.

Table 10.2   Essential Lessons Learned

Project Number	Project Title	Potential Lessons Learned	Best Practices
1	Patient engagement portal development	Balancing diverse needs may lead to feature bloat or overcomplexity.	Utilise DSDM prioritisation (MoSCoW) and agile sprints for focused development.
2	AI-assisted radiology tool	Failure to address explainability and bias can erode trust.	Invest in "explainable AI" techniques and rigorous testing with diverse data sets.
3	Redesigning a hospital unit workflow	Root cause may be social, not tech. Don't assume a software fix.	Deep process mapping in DSDM's foundations phase, and staff-led agile sprints.
4	Disease outbreak tracking	Balancing speed with accuracy, data quality may suffer initially.	Agile sprints to improve data validation alongside core functionality.
5	National clinical data repository	Governance battles can outweigh tech hurdles.	Extensive DSDM feasibility stage to build consensus, agile for tech iterations.

(Continued)

Table 10.2 (Continued)

Project Number	Project Title	Potential Lessons Learned	Best Practices
6	Telehealth for underserved populations	Ignoring socioeconomic barriers leads to unusable tools.	Empathy-driven user stories, sprints to overcome non-tech obstacles (like tech literacy).
7	Streamlining clinical trial processes	Inflexible systems stifle progress as regulations and protocols change.	Agile approach to integration with trial mgmt. vendors, APIs for adaptability.
8	Remote patient monitoring (heart failure)	Compliance hinges on more than just the device.	Agile sprints to improve ergonomics, personalisation of communication.
9	National adverse drug event reporting system	Lack of trust leads to underreporting, even with a slick interface.	Transparency in DSDM foundations, agile focuses on privacy-preserving features.
10	Precision medicine initiative	Lack of clarity on data use and ownership hinders collaboration.	Long DSDM feasibility phase on data standards, governance, and ethical use.
11	Mental health crisis response app	Prioritising safety is paramount, even if it means slower features roll-out.	DSDM timeboxing for core safety functions, agile feedback loops from mental health experts.
12	Supply chain optimisation for rural clinics	Tech alone won't fix unreliable infrastructure.	Local needs assessment in foundations, pilots of low-tech solutions alongside more advanced ones.
13	Rehabilitation game design	"Fun" can overshadow therapeutic goals if clinicians aren't deeply involved.	Clinician co-design in agile sprints, data collection on clinical outcomes.
14	Blockchain for medical supply chain	Regulatory landscape and industry buy-in are the real hurdles.	Extensive DSDM feasibility, agile pilots focused on proving value in a controlled network.
15	Social determinants of health data platform	Data without action is pointless.	DSDM focuses on outcomes, agile iterations on dashboards, and tools for intervention.

Project 1: Patient Engagement Portal Development

Potential pitfall: Attempting to be everything to everyone. Portals frequently become bloated with features that few patients utilise, reducing usability and raising maintenance costs.

Concrete lesson: Prioritisation is essential. Just because you can make something does not imply you should.

DSDM tie-in: The MoSCoW approach (must have, should have, could have, won't have) is crucial during the foundations phase to define the portal's scope.

Timeboxing forces developers to focus on essential features that are most valuable to the bulk of consumers.

Agile methodology involves short sprints and user testing to avoid focusing too much on niche functions.

A/B testing (multiple UI versions) can help developers determine what is genuinely intuitive for patients, rather than just what they think they need.

Project 2: AI-Assisted Radiology Tool

Potential pitfall: The "black box" issue. Even if a tool produces accurate diagnoses without explanations, it erodes practitioner trust, making adoption difficult.

Concrete lesson: Explainability must be built-in from the beginning. Accuracy isn't enough in healthcare.

DSDM tie-in: Prioritise stakeholder demands, such as radiologists' understanding of reasoning, at the foundations phase rather than as an afterthought.

Agile tie-in: Sprints concentrated on generating visualisation overlays or heatmaps to demonstrate which regions of the image drive AI decision-making.

Simulations and testing with physicians are required to fine-tune how this "explanation" is provided so that it is both informative and not unduly taxing.

Project 3: Designing a Hospital Unit Workflow

Potential pitfall: Choosing technology as the answer while neglecting underlying process inefficiencies or staff communication failures.

Concrete lesson: Before building any solution, it is critical to have a thorough awareness of the current situation, its pain points, and underlying reasons.

DSDM tie-in: The foundations phase focuses on thorough process mapping and workflow analysis. Don't go directly to solution brainstorming.

Agile tie-in: Observational sprints, such as shadowing staff to detect inefficiencies, can provide insights beyond interviews.

Trial-and-error mindset: Encourage experimenting with modest process adjustments (shift handover tweaks), gathering data, and iterating before investing in technology.

Project 4: Disease Outbreak Tracking

Potential pitfall: Prioritising data comprehensiveness over speed and usefulness during the early crisis response phase, resulting in slower decision-making.

Concrete lesson: In a fast-changing environment, "good enough" data that are available today are preferable to perfect data that arrive too late.

DSDM tie-in: Foundations are minimal yet vital. Defining primary data points is necessary for current action while realising that more will be required in the future.

Timeboxing and contingency: Initial rollouts prioritise ease of entry for people on the front lines, while concurrent timeboxes arrange for more advanced analytics.

Agile integration enables rapid prototyping of dashboards with relevant insights for decision-makers.

Flexibility in the data model allows for changes in case definitions or reporting requirements as the outbreak progresses.

Project 5: National Clinical Data Repository

Potential pitfall: Becoming mired down by the sheer magnitude and complexity of data harmonisation, governance, and ethical considerations, resulting in analysis paralysis.

Concrete lesson: Progress must be made gradually and incrementally. Success is dependent on demonstrating value quickly, even if only for a small portion of data or a specific disease area.

DSDM tie-in:

Extended feasibility phase: Long before coding begins, we map the landscape of stakeholders, rules, and current data sources.

Timeboxing and proof of concept: Prioritise one well-defined use case to establish feasibility before increasing ambition.

Agile methodology involves establishing data dictionaries, ontologies, and standards through sprints. This work is messy and would benefit from iteration.

Emphasis on researcher needs: Iterative development of the user interface (UI) guarantees that the repository is usable by the intended audience.

Project 6: Telehealth for Underserved Populations

Potential pitfall: Designing the solution in a vacuum, ignoring the social and economic constraints that patients in these regions may encounter.

Concrete lesson: Technology is simply one part of the puzzle. Success hinges on a thorough understanding of the target population's specific demands and limits.

DSDM tie-in: Foundations beyond technology – Conduct a thorough needs assessment involving community groups, social workers, and others. Understanding where non-technical problems occur.

Agile tie-in: Empathy-driven user stories (e.g., "As a patient with limited internet access, I need…") encourage non-technical development.

Flexibility in communication methods: Don't assume everyone has a smartphone or a good data connection. Sprints may prioritise SMS-based solutions or voice-only options.

Project 7: Streamline Clinical Trial Processes

Potential pitfall: Rigid systems that fail to adapt to changing trial protocols, regulatory changes, or the requirement to integrate data from new sources (wearables, for example).

Concrete lesson: Flexibility must be built into the solution to accommodate the inherent diversity of clinical research.

DSDM tie-in: Feasibility and foundations – Examine the present trial environment to find frequent places where delays arise due to inflexibility in current methods.

Avoid bespoke solutions. Timeboxing the assessment of whether off-the-shelf tools with customisation are preferable to creating from scratch.

Agile integration: Co-design with site sprints focused on feedback from research coordinators, who have a better grasp of where current processes cause bottlenecks.

API focus: Sprints to enable data sharing with external vendors (electronic case report form (eCRFs), etc.), anticipating the need to add new data sources as the trial landscape develops.

Project 8: Remote Patient Monitoring (Heart Failure)

Potential pitfall: Focusing only on the device's technical correctness and data collecting, while ignoring patient adherence and the burden of use.

Concrete lesson: Behavioural variables are as important as technology itself. A perfectly accurate technology will not enhance results unless patients use it on a regular basis.

DSDM tie-in: Foundations beyond technology – Learn about the daily life of the target patient population. Can people use the device easily, and how does it fit into their daily routine?

Timeboxing with a behavioural focus: Early timeboxes prioritised device ergonomics, simple setup instructions, and other standard performance measures.

Agile tie-in: Iterative device design – Rapid prototyping in sprints for feedback is especially useful when working with populations with low dexterity or technology skills.

Personalisation: Sprints focused on tailoring reminder frequency and alert escalation methods to specific patients.

Project 9: The National Adverse Drug Event Reporting System

Potential pitfall: Developing a technically sophisticated interface, yet adoption is hampered by a lack of confidence or concerns about time commitment amongst busy practitioners.

Concrete lesson: User incentives and demonstrating the value proposition are equally crucial as the tool's capabilities.

DSDM tie-in:

Thorough feasibility: Not simply "can we construct it," but 'will they use it'? Understanding the existing workflows and reporting constraints.

Transparency is essential: DSDM may organise explicit explanations of how data are used (and protected) to foster confidence from the start.

Agile integration: Sprints for user groups iteration on the interface to ensure simplicity of use for a wide range of users (clinicians from various specialisations, pharmacists, and the general public).

Collaboration with pharma: An agile strategy for connecting with their existing internal reporting systems, reducing the cost of duplicate data entry.

Project 10: Precision Medicine Initiative

Potential pitfall: Underestimating the scope of data standardisation and governance difficulties, resulting in useless, isolated data sets despite technological expertise.

Concrete lesson: Before diving into the fun task of algorithm creation, collaboration and consensus on data standards are required.

DSDM tie-in:

Extensive feasibility: Before coding begins, this project requires a thorough study of current data landscapes, privacy, cross-jurisdictional restrictions, and ethical concerns.

Governance reform: DSDM can help define decision-making structures and processes for prioritising research proposals and controlling access to the increasing data set.

Agile tie-ins include sprints for common vocabulary. Focused emphasis on creating ontologies and addressing differences in how various institutions code the same gene variant or clinical condition.

AI-focused teams: Sprints dedicated to developing algorithms that will detect trends in enormous data sets while also building trust in those algorithms.

Project 11: Mental Health Crisis Response App

Potential pitfall: Prioritising a diverse set of resources/tools over the immediate requirement for safety and triage within the app.

Concrete lesson: In a crisis, clarity and convenience of seeking support are critical. Too many choices can be bewildering and even dangerous.

DSDM tie-in: Prioritising safety – Features such as one-touch emergency escalation, geolocation sharing, and unambiguous protocols must be prioritised during the foundations phase.

Timeboxing for triage: Iterations of the initial evaluation algorithm or chatbot must involve tight communication with crisis line experts.

Agile tie-in: Privacy-focused sprints – Providing secure communication and data storage with clear explanations for consumers is crucial for building confidence.

Emphasis on user feedback: Mechanisms for in-the-moment and post-crisis feedback, as well as comprehensive analysis, to improve the experience and guarantee it is genuinely useful.

Project 12: Supply Chain Optimisation for Rural Clinics

Potential pitfall: Concentrating on cutting-edge "smart inventory" solutions while ignoring the realities of unreliable infrastructure and poor local technical assistance.

Concrete lesson: The most effective approach may be shockingly simple, with technology playing a supporting role.

DSDM tie-in: Through process analysis, DSDM can identify where failures occur. For example, expired medications owing to poor stock rotation are not the same as transportation delays.

Prioritisation based on impact: Forecasting based on past consumption data may be less effective than addressing frequent stockouts of vital prescriptions.

Agile integration: Frugal innovation – Sprints dedicated to testing simple systems (color-coded stock cards, SMS-based reordering) while also investigating more sophisticated alternatives.

Embrace local expertise: Clinic personnel are aware of the workarounds; sprints are designed to discover and then formalise best practices.

Project 13: Rehabilitation Game Design

Potential pitfall: Getting caught up in the 'coolness' of gamification, and not considering if the game corresponds with the basic features of therapeutic exercise required for recovery.

Concrete lesson: The design must be driven by clinical effectiveness rather than entertainment.

DSDM integration: Feasibility with therapists physical and occupational therapists must describe the necessary movements and feedback mechanisms, establishing limits for game developers.

Modular timeboxing: Breaking down development by body part (a hand rehab game followed by one focusing on balance) enables for more concentrated revisions.

Agile tie-in with patient feedback: Is the game pleasant and inspiring, or a chore? This feedback is vital.

Data collection focus: Sprints on how to effortlessly acquire correct motion data that therapists require for objective progress monitoring.

Project 14: Blockchain for the Medical Supply Chain

Potential pitfall: Overconfidence in technology. Obtaining buy-in from a fragmented industry and negotiating the complex regulatory landscape may be more difficult than blockchain implementation itself.

Concrete lesson: Stakeholder participation and a deep understanding of the existing ecosystem are required, not optional.

DSDM tie-in: Extensive feasibility – Identifying pain points, regulatory constraints (particularly for cross-border transactions), and computational expenses of blockchain at scale.

Timeboxing with pilots is focusing on a single, high-value medicine or device type within a confined network before attempting wider application.

Agile integration: User interface/user experience (UI/UX) for diverse users. Sprints focused on making the interface useable from manufacturers to front-line chemists while clarifying complex blockchain principles.

Interoperability challenges: Iterative techniques that allow data entry from many existing inventory systems, lowering adoption barriers.

Project 15: The Social Determinants of Health Data Platform

Potential pitfall: Collecting massive volumes of data without a clear strategy for converting it into focused interventions and resource allocation.

Concrete lesson: The purpose is not just to highlight discrepancies, but also to give tools for stakeholders to drive change.

DSDM tie-in: Stakeholder complexity – The foundations phase requires participation from agencies, health providers, and community organisations to describe the data's "so what."

Timeboxing by outcome: To show the notion, start with a single issue (food insecurity and health outcomes) and work your way up to larger issues.

Agile tie-in: Partnership sprints – Working with organisations on the ground will disclose current data that can be coupled with standard health measurements.

Creative data visualisation: Sprints focused on dashboards and tools that promote advocacy for policy changes, rather than just academic publications.

Conclusion

The Future of DSDM and Agile in Healthcare Project Management

While DSDM and agile methods provide useful frameworks for navigating the intricacies of healthcare projects, their future in this industry will be one of constant change and adaptation. Here's an overview of the trends and obstacles influencing their role:

The rise of AI: As AI-powered tools spread throughout healthcare, from algorithm-assisted diagnostics to drug discovery, project management must adapt. The emphasis on feasibility in DSDM merges with agile's emphasis on explainability and bias avoidance. Hybrid techniques will be required to deal with the technological and ethical challenges of AI initiatives.

Patient-centricity as the norm: Patients are becoming active participants in their own care. Stakeholder participation through DSDM and agile's user-centric design will be critical for developing solutions that actually meet and empower patients. This paradigm shift will be required for projects involving patient-generated data or technology-enabled home-based care.

Healthcare globalisation: Pandemics, the rush for breakthrough cures, and the search for cost-effective solutions are increasingly including cross-national collaborations. DSDM can provide the structured communication and decision-making processes required for global projects, whilst agile's adaptability facilitates the navigation of varied regulatory landscapes and cultural variances.

Focus on value: Healthcare systems are under pressure to show concrete results, not only complete projects on time and within budget. DSDM's emphasis on business value alignment, along with agile's capacity to pivot depending on KPIs, become critical for demonstrating the value of healthcare IT initiatives.

Beyond technology: DSDM and agile are increasingly being used to address larger healthcare concerns such as process improvement, public health campaigns, and the social determinants of health. Their emphasis on collaboration and outcome-oriented activity is ideal for these complicated challenges, where precise advance planning is unattainable.

DOI: 10.4324/9781032688435-14

The Path Forward

The most effective healthcare project managers of the future will not see a single technique as dogma. They will have a thorough understanding of the DSDM and agile principles, as well as healthcare domain expertise. Their hallmark will be flexibility in deploying the correct techniques at the right time, tailored to the specific project, organisational culture, and ever-changing healthcare sector.

The future belongs to healthcare project managers who

■ Embrace uncertainty: They understand that healthcare is fundamentally unpredictable and work to establish robust processes and adaptable mindsets within their workforce.
■ Encourage collaboration: They break down barriers, encouraging collaboration amongst clinicians, technologists, patients, and community stakeholders.
■ Maintain a constant emphasis on outcomes: Metrics matter, and demonstrating the impact of a project will be critical in securing buy-in and resources in a competitive healthcare climate.

Call to Action

This book has provided you with knowledge of DSDM and agile principles, as well as examples of how they are applied in healthcare. However, true learning occurs when these concepts are applied to real-world problems. Embrace innovation, learn from both successes and failures, and take an active role in building the future of healthcare project management.

Key Takeaways and Recommendations for Successful Implementation

Let's summarise the major insights and recommendations for successful implementation, which you can incorporate into your conclusion chapter.

Key Takeaways

Healthcare projects are unique: The intricacies of regulation, patient safety, and ethical concerns necessitate a nuanced approach to project management.

DSDM and agile are tools, not dogmas: The finest solutions frequently entail a careful balance of structure and adaptability, adapted to the unique project and circumstance.

Stakeholder engagement is vital: Clinicians, patients, administrators, and the larger community they serve all play a role in whether or not a project is successful.

Focus on outcomes, not just outputs: Did the initiative actually improve patient care, streamline operations, or advance research? Metrics demonstrating impact are vital.

Change is a constant: Healthcare is continually evolving; project management systems must be adaptable to rising technologies and changing laws.

Recommendations

Create a learning culture: Encourage your team to do constructive analysis of both accomplishments and failures. This promotes a culture of constant improvement.

Do not underestimate "soft skills": Effective communication, empathy, and the capacity to create trust with many stakeholders are just as important as technical project management skills.

Seek mentorship: Experienced healthcare project managers can help you avoid typical mistakes and adapt approaches to real-world scenarios.

Start small, showcase success: Early successes, especially on smaller projects, assist to boost confidence and buy-in for using DSDM and agile more broadly.

Become an advocate: Educate your organisation on the advantages of organised yet flexible project management. This is an investment in positive outcomes.

Let's take our case studies in Chapter 10 and tie them to the key takeaways to demonstrate those recommendations in a compelling way.

CASE STUDY 1

Patient Engagement Portal Development

The importance of stakeholder engagement cannot be overstated. Don't make assumptions about what users actually require. Early and ongoing communication with patients and physicians is critical to preventing feature bloat and ensuring the solution's effectiveness.

How the case makes it tangible: Assume the project was initially focused on appointment scheduling and lab result viewing but struggled with uptake. According to customer feedback, a secure chat capability with providers was a "must have" that drove utilisation. This emphasises the fact that the project team's concept of success may differ from that of the end users.

CASE STUDY 2

AI-Assisted Radiology Tool

Key takeaway: DSDM and agile are tools, not dogmas.

Recommendation: Projects using cutting-edge and potentially contentious technology require a combination of DSDM's upfront consideration of ethical concerns and agile's iterative approach to developing confidence through explainability and validation.

How the case makes it tangible: Assume if the only focus was on creating a highly accurate algorithm. However, it struggled with uptake because radiologists saw it as a "black box." A hybrid strategy, with early stages emphasising ethical considerations and incorporating tools to visualise the AI's decision-making alongside sprints for accuracy testing, would have been more effective.

CASE STUDY 3

Redesigning a Hospital Unit Workflow

The key takeaway: Change is the constant.

Recommendation: Develop an experimental mentality and empower front-line employees to identify and test small-scale process improvements. A culture of continual improvement is more flexible to the changing healthcare landscape than a single, large-scale redesign project.

How the case makes it tangible: Assume a huge IT revamp was implemented to improve communication but resulted in extra work for nurses, diverting them away from patient care. Smaller experiments (such as a trial of a new shift handover technique) would have allowed this detrimental influence to be discovered early and remedied.

CASE STUDY 4

Disease Outbreak Tracking

Key takeaway: Focus on outcomes, not just outputs.

Recommendation: In a quickly moving crisis, prioritise useable data and decision support tools over achieving flawless data completeness from the start. Balance the demand for speed with a long-term plan to improve data quality.

How the case makes it tangible: Assume the possibility that initial data collection efforts were so time-consuming that public health officials received hotspot notifications later. A pragmatic strategy, starting with a few key data points and adding more as the situation stabilised, would be more effective in achieving epidemic containment.

CASE STUDY 5

National Clinical Data Repository

Key takeaway: Healthcare projects are unique.

Large-scale, collaborative data initiatives require thorough feasibility assessments, as well as a focus on governance and data standardisation. Don't underestimate the time and work required to reach an agreement and handle privacy issues amongst varied stakeholders.

How the case makes it tangible: Assume a project that aimed to establish a technically advanced platform but encountered hurdles because academics couldn't agree on a shared language for a common condition, or patients were afraid to join owing to a lack of understanding about how their data would be utilised.

CASE STUDY 6

Telehealth for Underserved Populations

Key takeaway: Focus on outcomes, not just outputs.

Recommendation: Projects addressing complex social and economic hurdles cannot be measured only by the technological implementation of a telehealth platform. Metrics must also measure changes in access to care, health outcomes, and patient satisfaction amongst the target group.

How the case makes it tangible: Assume the project team was initially focused on the number of telehealth visits completed. However, further investigation revealed that, while some patients prospered, others experienced transportation challenges to appointments or struggled to purchase drugs. This demonstrates that the problem they were addressing was more than just video consultations; it required a more comprehensive strategy.

CASE STUDY 7

Streamlined Clinical Trial Procedures

The key takeaway: Change is the constant.

Recommendation: Include flexibility in the design of clinical trial systems. Use flexible architecture and prioritise integration capabilities to accommodate changing protocols, regulations, and the requirement to exchange data with new partners (e.g., wearable vendors).

How the case makes it tangible: Assume a strict eCRF (electronic case report form) system was deployed. However, a mid-trial protocol change required the gathering of additional data points, resulting in time-consuming workarounds and delays. A more adaptive system would have reduced the disruption.

CASE STUDY 8

Remote Patient Monitoring (Heart Failure)

Key takeaway: Stakeholder engagement is critical.

Recommendation: Device design and user experience are as important as technical precision in data collecting. Deep engagement between patients and their care teams is required to ensure that the solution fits into their life and meets their needs.

How the case makes it tangible: Assume the device was absolutely accurate, but patients with arthritis could difficulty put it on, or frequent warnings caused anxiety and a sense of constant surveillance. These ostensibly 'non-technical' concerns could jeopardise the project's success in improving patient outcomes.

CASE STUDY 9

The National Adverse Drug Event Reporting System

The key takeaway is to focus on outcomes rather than just outputs.

Recommendation: Success is dependent on making reporting easy and demonstrating its utility to busy practitioners. Connect the system directly to insights that enhance patient safety and reduce alert fatigue.

How the case makes it tangible: Assume a technology with a lovely interface that mostly creates reports for bureaucrats' inboxes. Compare that to a less spectacular technology that detects unexpected side effect clusters early on or sends clinicians personalised risk signals depending on their patients' previous prescriptions. The latter promotes adoption by addressing a pain point.

CASE STUDY 10

Precision Medicine Initiative

Key takeaway: DSDM and agile are tools, not dogmas.

Recommendation: This revolutionary project requires a lengthy feasibility phase (DSDM) to address the enormous scientific, ethical, and data governance concerns, as well as agile sprints aimed at building and validating the algorithms that will analyse the massive data sets.

How the case makes it tangible: Assume getting right into algorithm development only to learn that the methods used by various organisations to collect genetic data are so incompatible that the results are worthless. Alternatively, the focus is on the science, but patient privacy concerns undermine public trust. A balanced strategy addresses this.

CASE STUDY 11

The Mental Health Crisis Response App

Key takeaway: Stakeholder engagement is critical.

Recommendation: Prioritise safety and engagement with crisis line specialists from the start. Features like immediate emergency escalation and triage protocols demand equal attention as the app's overall user experience.

How the case makes it tangible: Assume a visually beautiful software with substantial self-help tools, but no obvious path for someone in an extreme suicidal crisis, might have disastrous repercussions. Early and continuing input from mental health professionals helps ensure that the app fulfils its intended goal.

CASE STUDY 12

Supply Chain Optimisation for Rural Clinics

Key takeaway: Healthcare projects are unique.

Focus on finding the fundamental cause of supply challenges and prioritising solutions that are appropriate for the local context and restrictions. Technology may play a role, but it is rarely the entire solution.

How the case makes it tangible: Assume adopting a "intelligent" inventory system that requires constant internet connectivity in an area with unpredictable power. A more effective option could be a combination of low-tech stock management tools and an emphasis on enhancing transportation reliability, even if it is less cutting-edge.

CASE STUDY 13

Rehabilitation Game Design

The key takeaway is to focus on outcomes rather than just outputs.

Recommendation: Work closely with physical and occupational therapists to ensure that the game mechanics are consistent with the therapeutic aims for each stage of recovery. The primary clinical goal should be supported rather than overshadowed by the entertainment value.

How the case makes it tangible: Assume a game with beautiful graphics and addictive gameplay, but the motions it encourages aren't appropriate for rehabilitation or are too challenging for people with limited mobility. Even if consumers like playing it, it will fail to achieve its fundamental goal.

CASE STUDY 14

Blockchain in Medical Supply Chains

Key takeaway: Healthcare projects are unique.

Building trust, managing rules, and achieving consensus within a dispersed system is frequently the main challenge, even when the technology is sound. Invest significant time in the early stages to engage stakeholders and identify their pain areas.

How the case makes it tangible: Assume if the blockchain trial exhibited tamper-proof monitoring, if it greatly increased chemist workload without addressing a problem they cared about, or if it violated medication import restrictions, the project would fail. This demonstrates that "cool" technology is not enough in healthcare.

CASE STUDY 15

Social Determinants of the Health Data Platform

Key takeaway: Stakeholder engagement is critical.

Recommendation: Collaborate with public health agencies, community groups, and healthcare practitioners from the start to define meaningful data points, plan interventions, and allocate resources. This forum should not only highlight problems but also serve as a catalyst for change.

How the case makes it tangible: Assume a dashboard that demonstrates stark inequalities in health outcomes by zip code. Without the support of people with the authority to change regulations, create clinics, or launch food assistance programmes, the effort is demoralising rather than revolutionary.

Encouragement for Healthcare Professionals to Embrace Agile Methods

Agile methods may appear to be a better fit for the fast-paced world of software development than for healthcare, which is highly regulated and safety-critical. However, agile's key concepts – collaboration, iteration, adaptability, and a focus on outcomes – have enormous potential to enhance how we deliver treatment, conduct research, and address systemic challenges in our healthcare systems.

Why Agile Matters to You

Break down silos: Agile promotes cross-functional teams. It provides physicians a say in developing the technology they use, allowing them to uncover inefficiencies and pain problems that project managers alone may overlook.

From frustration to solution: A continuous feedback loop and a willingness to pivot keep projects from drifting off track. Agile provides you with the skills to handle the "why does the system make me do this?!" issues with modest, targeted modifications.

Evidence-based improvement: Agile's emphasis on metrics and data-driven decision-making is consistent with healthcare's growing emphasis on quality and value. It enables you to demonstrate the tangible impact of an effort, so justifying future investment or changes.

Patient-centricity in action: Agile requires us to constantly ask, "Does this truly benefit the patient?" It is the antidote to solutions that benefit the IT department while increasing the workload of frontline employees.

Getting Started

You do not need to be a qualified scrum master to begin implementing agile thinking. Here's where to start:

Small wins, big impact: Identify a pain point in your department, such as a time-consuming documentation requirement or a communication breakdown that causes delays. Use agile-inspired tactics (rapid brainstorming sessions, brief pilots with many options) to address the issue, demonstrating the approach's benefits.

Find your allies: Most likely, there are others in your organisation who share your desire to enhance processes. Create a network of people interested in using agile methods and learning from one another's triumphs and challenges.

Language matters: Don't get caught up in jargon. Focus on translating agile concepts into healthcare terminology: "iteration" might be "testing and refining," and "sprints" can be "focused improvement cycles."

The Future of Healthcare Is Agile

As healthcare becomes more complex, individuals who value adaptation and a constant emphasis on improving outcomes will prosper. Agile techniques provide a road map for putting those attributes into practice. Join the campaign to enable healthcare workers to drive innovation rather than simply using inflexible technology and obsolete methods.

It Is Time to Take Charge

Don't wait for someone to provide you with the ideal solution. The agile mentality empowers you to be the change you wish to see in healthcare. Here's how to start a change in your own environment:

Question everything. From how your clinic arranges appointments to how quality indicators are published, ask "why do we do it this way?" and challenge the belief that it cannot be changed.

Prove the concept: Instead of requesting a large system redesign, gain support for a brief, focused experiment. Use agile-style data collection and rapid feedback loops to show how even little changes can bring significant benefits.

Share your success. Do not let agile become your hidden weapon. Evangelise the victories! Showcase how this approach of thinking helped you enhance patient care, streamline operations, and progress research.

The Transformation Starts With You

Those who refuse to accept the existing quo will be the ones who shape the future of healthcare. Agile is not a panacea, but it does create a framework for continuous improvement, empowers frontline physicians to lead innovation, and guarantees that every change, every iteration, serves the ultimate objective of providing better, more compassionate, and more effective care to the patients we serve.

Index

Note: The page numbers in *italics* and **bold** denotes figures and tables, respectively.